THE BIBLE COMPASS

A Catholic's Guide to Navigating the Scriptures

EDWARD SRI

ASCENSION PRESS

West Chester, Pennsylvania

Nihil obstat: William C. Beckman, M.T.S.
        Censor Librorum

Imprimatur: +Most Reverend Charles J. Chaput, O.F.M. Cap.
        Archbishop of Denver
        July 16, 2009

Ascension Press
Post Office Box 1990
West Chester, PA 19380
Orders: 1-800-376-0520
www.AscensionPress.com
www.BibleStudyforCatholics.com

Cover design: Devin Schadt

Printed in the United States of America
10 11 12 13 14 8 7 6 5 4 3 2

ISBN 978-1-934217-78-8

To Curtis Martin,
In gratitude for years of friendship
while studying and proclaiming God's Word together.
1 Thessalonians 2:8

CONTENTS

Biblical Abbreviations

The following abbreviations are used for the various Scriptural verses cited throughout the book. (Note: CCC = *Catechism of the Catholic Church*.)

Old Testament

Gn	Genesis
Ex	Exodus
Lv	Leviticus
Nm	Numbers
Dt	Deuteronomy
Jos	Joshua
Jgs	Judges
Ru	Ruth
1 Sam	1 Samuel
2 Sam	2 Samuel
1 Kgs	1 Kings
2 Kgs	2 Kings
1 Chr	1 Chronicles
2 Chr	2 Chronicles
Ezr	Ezra
Neh	Nehemiah
Tb	Tobit
Jdt	Judith
Est	Esther
1 Mc	1 Maccabees
2 Mc	2 Maccabees
Jb	Job
Ps	Psalms
Prv	Proverbs
Eccl	Ecclesiastes
Sng	Song of Songs
Wis	Wisdom
Sir	Sirach
Is	Isaiah
Jer	Jeremiah
Lam	Lamentations
Bar	Baruch
Ez	Ezekiel
Dn	Daniel
Hos	Hosea
Jl	Joel
Am	Amos
Ob	Obadiah
Jon	Jonah
Mi	Micah
Na	Nahum
Hb	Habakkuk
Zep	Zephaniah
Hg	Haggai
Zec	Zechariah
Mal	Malachi

New Testament

Mt	Matthew
Mk	Mark
Lk	Luke
Jn	John
Acts	Acts
Rom	Romans
1 Cor	1 Corinthians
2 Cor	2 Corinthians
Gal	Galatians
Eph	Ephesians
Phil	Philippians
Col	Colossians
1 Thess	1 Thessalonians
2 Thess	2 Thessalonians
1 Tm	1 Timothy
2 Tm	2 Timothy
Ti	Titus
Phlm	Philemon
Heb	Hebrews
Jas	James
1 Pt	1 Peter
2 Pt	2 Peter
1 Jn	1 John
2 Jn	2 John
3 Jn	3 John
Jude	Jude
Rv	Revelation

ACKNOWLEDGMENTS

I am grateful to Curtis Mitch and Mary Healy, who offered feedback on some sections of this work. I also am thankful for my many colleagues and students at the Augustine Institute, Benedictine College, and the Fellowship of Catholic University Students (FOCUS) who have explored the Bible with me in various settings over the past decade. Our study, discussions, and prayer together have helped deepen my understanding of the mystery of divine revelation and the Scriptures in particular. Many of those shared insights have worked their way into this book. Finally, I express deep gratitude to my wife, Elizabeth, and our children for their prayers and encouragement throughout the labor of this work.

INTRODUCTION

For as the rain and the snow come down from heaven, and do not return there but water the earth, making it bring forth and sprout, giving seed to the sower and bread to the eater, so shall my word be that goes forth from my mouth; it shall not return to me empty, but it shall accomplish that which I purpose, and prosper in the thing for which I sent it. – Isaiah 55:10-11

God's inspired words in the Bible have the power to change lives dramatically. When a fourth-century man named Anthony walked into a church during Mass, he heard the following words from the Gospel: "If you would be perfect, go, sell what you possess and give to the poor, and you will have treasure in heaven" (Mt 19:21). Moved, Anthony sold all his possessions, gave the money to the poor, and eventually became the great hermit and patriarch of monastic life, St. Anthony of the Desert (c. 251–356).

When a young man named Augustine found himself intellectually convinced of Christianity but unable to free himself from his sexual sins and convert to the Catholic faith, he opened up the Scriptures to a passage in Romans that calls readers to "put on the Lord Jesus Christ, and make no provision for the flesh, to gratify its desires" (Rom 13:14). Though Augustine's conversion was a long, gradual process, his encounter with this biblical text unlocked something for him spiritually and had an immediate effect: "For in an instant," he later wrote, "... it was as though the light of confidence flooded into my heart and all the darkness of doubt was dispelled."[1] At that moment, Augustine finally committed himself to the Christian life, and he eventually became a great bishop, saint, and Doctor of the Church.

Not all Christians can expect to have an extraordinary encounter with the Scriptures like Sts. Anthony and Augustine. Nevertheless, the Bible is meant to be read as a personal word from God to each of us, experienced as a word that touches our souls, shapes our lives, and leads us into ever deeper union with the Lord and his Church. As Vatican II taught, "In the sacred books, the Father who is in heaven comes lovingly to meet his children, and talks with them."[2]

But do we truly experience the Scriptures in such an intimate way? *The Bible Compass* seeks to assist readers who sincerely desire to understand the Bible and know God better through the sacred books but are uncertain about how to begin studying the Scriptures effectively. In addition, this book will address the many questions readers of the Bible face today and equip them with the background and the practical steps they need for their own personal journey through the Bible. My hope is that, armed with this background, readers might find greater confidence and clarity in studying the Bible and that they may encounter the Lord and their Catholic faith more deeply when reading the Scriptures.

On a basic level, this book will address common, fundamental questions about the Bible itself: What does it mean that the Bible is inspired by God? What is the relationship between Sacred Scripture, Sacred Tradition, and the Church's Magisterium? We also will consider questions about the Bible's origins and development: How did the early Church determine which writings were part of the New Testament canon, and how did the Church view other writings, such as the gnostic gospels? How did the Old Testament canon come to be, and why do Catholics have the seven deuterocanonical books that most Protestant Bibles leave out? And, finally,

---

[1]   St. Augustine, *Confessions,* Book VIII, Chapter 12, par. 29.
[2]   *Dei Verbum* (DV) 21; see CCC 105-106.

questions about the Bible's trustworthiness (i.e., in what sense is the Bible without error) will also be addressed.

Five Keys for Interpreting the Bible

Second, this book will provide readers with five keys for interpreting the Bible correctly. These principles are based on the teachings from the *Catechism of the Catholic Church* and are indispensable for any Catholic desiring to read the Scriptures from the heart of the Church. The five interpretive keys are the following:

- *First Key:* Discover the Author's Intention (CCC 109-110)
- *Second Key:* Be Attentive to the Unity of Scripture (CCC 112)
- *Third Key:* Read Scripture within the Living Tradition of the Church (CCC 113)
- *Fourth Key:* Read Scripture within the Symphony of God's Revelation (CCC 114)
- *Fifth Key:* Use the Four Senses of Scripture (CCC 115-119)

These five keys not only help ensure that our reading of the Bible stays on the right track but also serve as lights on our path, illuminating our understanding of the Scriptures so that we can seek Jesus Christ in the sacred texts—or, in the words of Pope Benedict XVI, "Look for the Word within the words."[3]

In addition, this book will open up the biblical world for readers, acquainting them with the Dead Sea Scrolls, Josephus, ancient rabbinic writings, and biblical maps to show how archaeology, geography, and history can shed light on our understanding of the Scriptures. We will also walk through the twelve periods of biblical history, tracing the development of God's plan of salvation from the Old Covenant into the New and connecting each of the

---

[3]   Pope Benedict XVI, *Address at the Opening of the 12ᵗʰ Ordinary General Assembly of the Synod of Bishops* (October 6, 2008).

Bible's seventy-three books with their corresponding periods. With a general grasp of the "big picture" of Sacred Scripture, readers will have a framework for understanding how the many "smaller" biblical stories fit together in the one drama of God's plan of salvation.

Finally, we will conclude by offering an introduction to the resources, translations, and methods commonly used for Scripture study, as well as some reflections on how to pray with the Bible using the traditional method of *lectio divina*.

In sum, *The Bible Compass* is meant to serve as a basic handbook for Catholics in their study of the Sacred Scriptures, addressing common questions they have about the Bible and equipping them with practical guides for reading and interpreting the sacred books. In order to make the Church's teachings about Scripture more readily accessible to lay readers, we will quote from Vatican II's *Dogmatic Constitution on Divine Revelation (Dei Verbum)* and other sources as they appear in the *Catechism of the Catholic Church*. Moreover, while we will draw on biblical scholarship to elucidate certain points, it is beyond the scope of this book to enter into the current scholarly debate on the various topics addressed. Rather, our goal here is to simplify the many relevant issues regarding hermeneutics, canonicity, divine revelation, and biblical history for the average Catholic who wants to know and study the Bible better.

– Edward Sri
Denver
Holy Week, 2009

PART I

DIVINE REVELATION:
THE UNVEILING OF GOD

CHAPTER 1

Is the Bible Really Inspired by God?

The Bible is often considered "the greatest book ever written." At first glance, however, it does not appear to be a book at all. It looks more like a library, for it is a collection of seventy-three different books authored by many different people over the course of many centuries. These books were written from various locations to diverse audiences and in three different languages (i.e., Hebrew, Aramaic, and Greek). Moreover, the seventy-three books of the Bible reflect a wide range of literary genres: historical narrative, poetry, proverbial sayings, genealogies, personal letters, laws, and prophecy, for example.

So why do we consider these many, varied works to be a single great book? Because they each have one very important thing in common—namely, a common author, God. And it is this divine author who, through these varied books of the Bible, tells one overarching story—the drama of his plan of salvation.

This point is made in the *Catechism of the Catholic Church*, which teaches that God is the author of Sacred Scripture. The books of the Bible were inspired by God's Holy Spirit. The English word "inspiration" is based on the Greek word *theópneustos*, which translated literally means "God-breathed" (2 Tm 3:16; see CCC 105). Thus, when Christians speak of the Scriptures as being

inspired, this means that the Holy Spirit influenced human writers
such as Matthew, Mark, and Luke to write not just their own words
but God's words in the Scriptures. In other words, God "breathed"
his own divine word through the words of men.

This does not mean God is the only author of Scripture but rather
that he is its primary author. Christianity has always recognized that
human authors were involved in the writing of the Bible as well.
Men such as Sts. Peter and Paul composed the sacred books and
acted as true authors under divine inspiration. The human writers
made full use of their own freedom, creativity, and writing style to
communicate their message to their particular audiences.

Like Christ: Human and Divine

How, then, did the Holy Spirit influence the human writers of
Scripture? The profound interaction between God's inspiration and
the human author's writing remains somewhat of a mystery. But
the Church has shed some light on the matter. On the one hand, we
must affirm the human authorship of Scripture. The sacred writers
were not passively writing like mechanical robots, making no
personal contribution to the text of Scripture. The Second Vatican
Council explains that the sacred writers acted as "true authors,"
using their own powers and abilities and employing particular
literary forms, styles, and modes of narrating that were common
in their time.[4] Therefore, interpreters of the Bible "should carefully
investigate what meaning the sacred writers really intended, and
what God wanted to manifest by means of their word."[5]

On the other hand, we must hold to the divine authorship of
Scripture. God truly is the author of the Old and New Testament
books "whole and entire, with all their parts."[6] He did not inspire
only certain sections of the Bible. Neither did he merely prevent the

---

[4]   CCC 106, 110, citing DV 11-12.
[5]   CCC 109, citing DV 12.
[6]   See CCC 105, citing DV 11.

human writers from falling into error. In such a limited view, God would be more like an editor who helps the writer avoid making mistakes than a real author. Instead, the Church teaches that God positively influenced the writing of the text; thus, the words of Scripture are truly God's words. Vatican I made this point, teaching that the Church holds these books as sacred and canonical, not because "they contain revelation without error; but because, having been written by the inspiration of the Holy Spirit, they have God as their author and, as such, they have been handed down to the Church itself."[7]

It also would be a mistake to see inspiration as merely the subsequent approval of a text by the Church. According to this view, the individual books of the Bible were written in a purely human way, but later, when they were accepted by the Church as authoritative and received into the canon of Scripture, they came to be considered channels of God's revelation. In this flawed perspective, however, God is not a true author. He is more like a government official who has his public relations staff craft his speeches for him but who is not truly involved in the writing process itself. As Vatican I taught, "The Church holds these books as sacred and canonical, not because, having been put together by human industry alone, they were then approved by its authority." Rather, the Church accepts these books as part of the canon of Scripture because they were "written by the inspiration of the Holy Spirit" and thus "they have God as their author."[8]

In conclusion, the Bible is like Jesus Christ himself: fully human and fully divine. With the mystery of divine inspiration, it is precisely through each human author's own particular personality, freedom, and skills that God communicated what he wanted written in the books of the Bible. The human writer's intention concurs perfectly with the divine will. As the *Catechism* explains,

---

[7] Vatican I, *Dei Filius (Dogmatic Constitution on the Catholic Faith)*, chapter 2 (DS, 1787).
[8] Ibid.

"To compose the sacred books, God chose certain men who, all the while he employed them in this task, made full use of their own faculties and powers so that, though he acted in them and by them, it was as true authors that they consigned to writing whatever he wanted written and no more."[9]

But Is God Really the Author of the Bible?

God did not leave us on our own to find him and figure out the meaning of our lives by ourselves. He lovingly chose to communicate himself to us and reveal his plan for us. One of the main ways he did this was through the Bible.

It is understandable, though, that some people today may find the idea of God inspiring human beings to write the Bible difficult to grasp. This is probably because many people do not really believe that God interacts in the world at all—a popular view known as *deism*. A deist believes there is a God but does not believe this God has any personal involvement in this world or our lives. So, if one doesn't truly believe in a God who has a plan for us, knows our thoughts, hears our prayers, performs miracles, or interacts in the world at all, then, of course, he or she is not going to be very open-minded about the possibility of God communicating to us through the Bible.

But it simply doesn't make sense to limit God in this radical way. If there is a God who created the world, he should be able to interact in the world that he created. No one would say that a builder who constructed a large building is incapable of entering his building and talking to the people inside it. Similarly, if God created the universe, then he, as the divine builder of the cosmos, is certainly capable of acting within the very world he made. Therefore, we should be open to the fact that God at least has the ability to hear our prayers, influence affairs on earth, work miracles, and even communicate to us through inspired human writers. It would be completely unreasonable to say that he doesn't.

---

[9] CCC 106, citing DV 11.

Furthermore, God not only has the ability to communicate with us. It makes sense that he actually would. After all, we need his help to understand him and his plan for our lives. St. Thomas Aquinas explains that our finite minds by themselves cannot fully grasp the infinite God. Many of us have a hard enough time understanding the things of this world, such as physics, calculus, or molecular biology. If we experience difficulty understanding such earthly matters, we should not be surprised that our limited minds on their own cannot understand God. Since God is infinite and our minds are finite, it seems fitting that God would reveal himself to us and communicate his will to us so that we could know, love, and serve him more fully. This is what he has done through the Bible (and Sacred Tradition, but more on that a bit later).

CHAPTER 2

Scripture, Tradition, and the Magisterium

God's revelation is intensely personal. It is not a word spoken long ago that remains locked up in the past. It is not a series of teachings, principles, and prophecies merely to be understood and followed. Rather, it is the intimate self-disclosure of our God, who seeks us out and makes himself known to us so that we can ever more respond to him in a relationship of love.

This chapter will lay important foundations for understanding the Church's teachings on divine revelation. We will first look at how God reveals himself to us and how this revelation has been passed on faithfully from Jesus Christ and the apostles to us today. Here, we also will see how more than the Bible is necessary to know and understand all that God has revealed. In addition to Scripture, Sacred Tradition and the Church's teaching office (the Magisterium) are essential for knowing God's word. What is Tradition? What is the Magisterium? And why do we need these to understand Scripture? These are some of the many fundamental issues that we will explore in this chapter.

Faith and Reason

The *Catechism* begins its treatment on divine revelation by noting how there are "two orders of knowledge"—two ways we can know reality. On the one hand, God gave us natural reason. Through our human intellects, we can know many things. With sound reasoning, we can come to know that 2 + 2 = 4. We can discover how the earth revolves around the sun and learn to build bridges, airplanes, and rockets. Through our human reason alone—apart from the Bible or the Church—we also can come to know certain moral principles, such as the fact that murder and stealing are wrong. We can even come to know through human reason that there must be a God who created the world.

But the *Catechism* goes on to explain that there is a second order of knowledge "which man cannot possibly arrive at by his own powers." This is called "the order of divine Revelation."[10] Divine revelation enables us to know many things about God and his plan for us that we could not know by reason alone. For example, sound reasoning might lead one to the conclusion that there must be a God, but no sage or philosopher, by reason alone, ever came up with the notion that God exists as Father, Son, and Holy Spirit. The Holy Trinity was revealed to us by Jesus Christ and explained by the Church over the centuries. Likewise, while man does not need the Bible or the Church to know that God exists, reason alone could not conclude that this God would become man and die for our sins. The Incarnation was revealed to us by God through his Son, Jesus Christ.

These revealed truths are called mysteries of faith. Though this word sounds "mysterious," we should not think that the mysteries of Christianity require purely blind leaps of intellectual faith, as if reason were completely tossed out the window when one enters the realm of Christian belief. Faith and reason are meant to go together. Mysteries of the faith like the Trinity and the Incarnation go beyond what human reason could fully grasp, but they are not opposed to reason. In fact, they are eminently reasonable.

---

10   CCC 50.

The Back of the Book

By way of analogy, we can think of the mysteries of faith revealed to us by Christ as somewhat like the answers in the back of the book. In junior high, I struggled with math. When I went off to high school, I remember being nervous on the first day of my freshman math class. This was high school algebra, and I was going to be stretched like never before in my mathematical abilities. Our teacher handed out our textbooks, and I cringed as I flipped through the pages, where I found strange symbols, letters, and numbers thrown together in all sorts of equations that were completely new to me. But then, at the back of the book, I discovered something I had never seen before. To my amazement (and great joy!), the back of my math textbook included the answers to all of the odd numbered questions in the book. I suddenly realized that I now at least had a chance to pass high school algebra. For every homework assignment, I would be starting off with at least fifty percent of the answers correct!

Why do textbook publishers put the answers to the odd-numbered questions in the back of the book? It is certainly not to help students cheat by giving them a fifty-percent start. The answers are given not only so that students can check if their work is correct, but also to help students when they are struggling to solve a math problem. With the answer revealed, the student can "work backward" and figure out how to arrive at the right answer.

Of course, divine revelation is quite different from the answers in the back of a textbook. But at least in this sense, there may be a similarity: When God reveals a mystery of faith that is beyond our full comprehension, we can apply our mind to the mystery and begin to see its reasonableness. Thus, while human reason on its own could never come up with the idea of God being three divine Persons possessing one divine nature, once the doctrine of the Trinity is revealed, our reason can "work backward," aided by the light of faith, and begin to see that this doctrine is not contrary to reason but is, actually, reasonable.

The Unveiling of God

Next, the *Catechism* addresses the "what," "why," and "how" about divine revelation itself.

First, the *Catechism* discusses the question of "what": What does God reveal? "It pleased God, in his goodness and wisdom, to reveal himself and to make known the mystery of his will."[11] Notice that the *Catechism* doesn't say God reveals Bible stories, doctrines, or moral codes. Rather, God reveals *himself*. This tells us that divine revelation is not merely about passing on information— abstract dogmas to believe and theoretical principles to follow. Divine revelation is something much more intensely personal. It is God's intimate disclosure of himself. In fact, the Greek word for revelation *(apokalypsis)* means an "uncovering," "unveiling," or "disclosure." Like a bride unveiling herself to her bridegroom, God lovingly discloses himself to his people. All the doctrines and moral precepts of the Church must be seen as bearing witness to this loving self-communication of God, as aspects of his intimate unveiling of his face to us.

Second, the *Catechism* addresses the question of "why": Why does God reveal himself? "God … wants to communicate his own divine life to the men he freely created, in order to adopt them as his sons in his only-begotten Son."[12] Here, we see that divine revelation is profoundly relational. God reveals in order to invite us into an intimate relationship with him as our heavenly Father. The main purpose of divine revelation, therefore, is not to provide us with a lot of good religious information and make us smart Christians. God reveals himself not to make us theologians but to make us his children. As the *Catechism* explains, God unveils himself and his plan to us so that we will respond to him in love. "By revealing himself God wishes to make [us] capable of responding to him, and

---

11   CCC 51, citing DV 2.
12   CCC 52.

of knowing him, and of loving him far beyond [our] own natural capacity."[13]

A man who holds all the right doctrines and memorizes the *Catechism* is not a good Christian if he does not respond to God's revelation with love, entrusting his life to the Lord and following his commands. While orthodoxy—right doctrine—is absolutely essential for the Christian life, it is not enough. Right doctrine is meant to lead to right living. Indeed, all the truths God reveals—the doctrines, moral principles, and ways of life and worship—are meant to be life-transforming, leading us to holiness and equipping us to grow in love.

The Divine Pedagogy

Finally, the *Catechism* addresses the question of "how": How does God reveal himself? First, God reveals "by deeds and words."[14] When thinking about God's revelation to humanity, we might envision certain dramatic, revelatory moments such as God giving the Ten Commandments on Mount Sinai, God calling Moses at the burning bush, or the heavenly voice at Christ's baptism, saying, "This is my beloved Son, with whom I am well pleased" (Mt 3:17; see Lk 3:22). However, the *Catechism* teaches that God communicates not only through his words but also through his actions in history. And sometimes, his actions speak louder than his words. For example, God may say that he loves his people Israel, but he reveals his love for the Israelites even more powerfully through his actions in the Exodus, hearing their cry for help, liberating them from their suffering as slaves in Egypt, and leading them to the Promised Land. In the same way, Jesus may teach in the Sermon on the Mount, saying, "Love your enemies and pray for those who persecute you" (Mt 5:44), but he communicates that message even more powerfully when he embodies it by forgiving his own enemies

---

[13] CCC 52.

[14] CCC 53, citing DV 2.

during the crucifixion, saying, "Father, forgive them, they know not what they do" (Lk 23:34). Therefore, we should pay close attention not only to the words of God spoken through his mediators, prophets, and apostles, but also to his actions in salvation history, for God communicates in words and deeds.

In addition, God "communicates himself to man gradually." God is the perfect teacher, revealing the right thing at the right time for his people. Throughout the Old Testament, God prepared Israel and humanity for the coming of Christ. He unveiled himself in stages through Abraham, Moses, David, and the prophets, disclosing more of his plan of salvation step by step.

This divine revelation culminated in the person of Jesus Christ.[15] Jesus is not just a teacher, prophet, or a messenger sent on behalf of a distant deity who remains far removed from our lives. Jesus is God himself who became man and dwelt among us. As the Letter to the Hebrews begins, "In many and various ways God spoke of old to our fathers by the prophets; but in these last days he has spoken to us by a Son" (Heb 1:1-2). As the God-man, Jesus himself is the fullness of divine revelation. His entire life—his words and deeds—is the fullness of God's unveiling of himself to the human family. Since revelation is complete in Christ, no new public revelation is to be expected before the Second Coming of Christ at the end of time.[16]

---

[15]   CCC 53.

[16]   Regarding "private" revelations, the *Catechism* explains that some of these have been recognized by the authority of the Church, but even these do not belong to the deposit of faith that all Christians must hold. "It is not their role to improve or complete Christ's definitive Revelation, but to help live more fully by it in a certain period of history" (CCC 67). The Church does not accept so-called "revelations" of various sects that claim to surpass or "correct" Christ's revelation (see CCC 67).

From Christ to the Church: Scripture, Tradition, and the Magisterium

This divine revelation summed up in Christ was meant to be passed on to subsequent generations and proclaimed to all of humanity. After his resurrection, Jesus told the apostles, "Go, therefore, and make disciples of all nations, baptizing them in the name of the Father and of the Son and of the Holy Spirit, teaching them to observe all that I have commanded you" (Mt 28:19-20). Christ's apostles and their successors began to fulfill this "Great Commission" by handing on the revelation of Christ in two ways: orally and in writing.[17]

The oral form of passing on the Gospel is known as Sacred Tradition, while the written form refers to Sacred Scripture. Both Scripture and Tradition are entrusted to the Church's Magisterium, or teaching authority, as the authentic guardian and interpreter of the heritage of faith passed on from the time of the apostles to the present day. Like the three legs of a tripod, Scripture, Tradition, and the Magisterium are each needed to know and understand God's revelation. As Vatican II taught, "It is clear, therefore, that in the supremely wise arrangement of God, sacred Tradition, Sacred Scripture, and the Magisterium of the Church are so connected and associated that one of them cannot stand without the others. Working together, each in its own way, under the action of the one Holy Spirit, they all contribute effectively to the salvation of souls."[18]

We will look at Scripture, Tradition, and the Magisterium in more detail in other sections of this book, but here is a brief introduction to these concepts:

Sacred Scripture. Christ's message of salvation was put into writing by some of the apostles and their associates. These sacred authors, along with the authors of the Old Testament books, wrote in a human way, making full use of their own abilities and

---

[17] CCC 76.
[18] See CCC 95, citing DV 10.

writing styles, with their original audience in mind. But under the inspiration of the Holy Spirit, they "consigned to writing whatever he wanted written, and no more."[19] Thus, the Scriptures truly have God as their author as well. Indeed, the Scriptures are the words of God in the words of man. "For in the sacred books, the Father who is in heaven meets his children with great love and speaks with them."[20] (For more on the inspiration of Scripture and its unique role in God's revelation, review Chapter 1.)

Sacred Tradition. Long before the New Testament Scriptures about Christ were ever written, the apostles were already setting out to fulfill the Great Commission. From the beginning of the Church at Pentecost, they were passing on the revelation of Christ and inviting people into communion with him (see Acts 2-5). In these earliest years of the Church, the Gospel was handed on through various unwritten means: through their preaching, their example, and the institutions they established. Each of these means embodied a living tradition—a whole way of life—that the apostles received directly from living with Christ and from the prompting of his Holy Spirit.[21] St. Paul himself commands his followers to observe not only the written form of his teaching, but also the oral traditions he passed on: "Stand firm and hold to the traditions which you were taught by us, either by word of mouth or by letter" (2 Thess 2:15). The Holy Spirit guides this living transmission of the Christian faith throughout the centuries, as the faith is passed on from generation to generation through the Church's doctrine, life, and worship.[22] (For more on Sacred Tradition—what it is, where we find it, and the crucial role it plays in interpreting Scripture correctly—see Chapter 5.)

The Magisterium. The great heritage of faith contained in Scripture and Tradition was handed down from the apostles

---

[19] CCC 106.
[20] DV 21.
[21] CCC 76, citing DV 7.
[22] CCC 78.

and entrusted to the teaching office of the Church, called the Magisterium. The Magisterium consists of the apostles' successors (the bishops) teaching in union with the successor of St. Peter (the pope). They are the only authoritative interpreters of the word of God. However, we should not think of the Magisterium as a separate *source* of divine revelation, but as the guardian and protector of the divine revelation contained in Scripture and Tradition. The Magisterium is "not superior to the word of God, but is its servant."[23] Assisted by the Holy Spirit, the Church's Magisterium "listens to this devotedly, guards it with dedication, and expounds it faithfully."[24] We will discuss the Magisterium in greater detail in Chapter 6.

---

[23] CCC 86, citing DV 10.
[24] Ibid.

PART II

Five Keys for Interpreting
Scripture Correctly

Introduction to Part II

When explaining a Scriptural passage from a Catholic perspective, I have occasionally had people ask me, "But isn't that just *your* interpretation of the Bible?" Such a question is understandable. With countless Christians drawing diverse conclusions from the same sacred text, some people might get the impression that the Bible has no real, intrinsic meaning that applies to everyone. Every reader imposes his own views onto the text and draws his own conclusions. Baptists interpret the Bible one way, Lutherans another, Methodists yet another, etc. Given this state of affairs, is there any way to know whether one's interpretation is correct?

We will see that the Bible may have many layers of spiritual meaning, speaking to various individuals and situations in different ways today. But at the same time, biblical interpretation is not meant to be a completely open-ended, free-for-all affair. Since the Bible's human writers intended to communicate something specific to their audiences, there is an objective meaning of Scripture in its original literal-historical sense. Even the personal, spiritual application one might draw from a particular verse or passage needs to be carried out within certain parameters. The Holy Spirit who inspired the human writers of Scripture continues to work in the life of the Church today. Therefore, the Catholic Church teaches that reading Scripture in the same Spirit in which it was written is also crucial for interpreting the Bible properly. As the *Catechism* explains, "To interpret Scripture correctly, the reader must be attentive to what the human authors truly wanted to affirm and to what God wanted to reveal to us by their words."[25]

In Part II, we will explore five keys for interpreting Scripture correctly—five interpretive principles that come right from the *Catechism* and reflect the way the great saints, theologians, and Doctors of the Church have approached the Bible throughout the ages. These five keys will help us unlock the meaning of the Bible and discover the treasures God has in store for us personally in the Scriptures.

---

[25]   CCC 109.

CHAPTER 3

The First Key: Discover the Author's Intention

Have you ever been in conversation with someone who is not a good listener? The other person may think he understands you, but he really is not paying close attention to what you are trying to communicate. Maybe he only hears part of what you are saying. Maybe he even cuts you off before you finish your sentence. Perhaps he is too quick to relate everything you say back to his own experience or ideas. Talking to someone who listens poorly can be quite frustrating!

We want to be good listeners of God's words to us in the Bible, and that means we must pay close attention to what he is trying to communicate. Since God speaks to us in a human way through human writers, the first principle for biblical interpretation given in the *Catechism* is to consider the intention of the human author. "To interpret Scripture correctly, the reader must be attentive to what the human authors truly wanted to affirm and to what God wanted to reveal to us by their words."[26]

We must remember that Scripture was written by real human beings who had a particular audience in mind and a particular message they wanted to communicate to that audience. When we interpret the Bible in a vacuum—when we fail to consider the human

---

[26] CCC 109.

writer's intention, historical setting, and audience—we may not fully
grasp the original meaning of the biblical passage we are reading.

Take, for example, the book of Revelation's portrayal of Jesus as
a lion and a lamb.[27] Reading this passage at face value, some well-
intentioned Christians might conclude that the Bible here is depicting
Jesus as strong and merciful. Jesus is powerful, like a lion, but he
also is kind and gentle, like a lamb. While Jesus Christ is indeed the
omnipotent Lord who is mercifully gentle with us, this is not the main
point Revelation 5 is making. The images of a lion and a lamb had a
particular meaning to the author of Revelation and his audience. In
light of the Old Testament (which the book of Revelation constantly
draws upon), the image of a lion would recall the royal blessing given
to the tribe of Judah. When the patriarch Jacob blessed his son Judah
in Genesis 49, he described him as "a lion's whelp" and foretold how
a royal scepter (symbol of a king) would not depart from the line of
Judah. This king not only will reign over the other tribes of Israel
(who "will bow down before" him), but also will have an international
influence, as the other nations will obey him (Gn 49:8-12). Since
the image of a lion in the Old Testament was linked with these royal
hopes for the Jewish people, Jesus' appearance in Revelation 12 as
a "lion" signals that he is the great king from the tribe of Judah for
whom Israel has been yearning. He is the ultimate fulfillment of the
prophecy of Genesis 49.

Similarly, the lamb is not mentioned in Revelation 5 to bring
to mind a cute, cuddly animal. Rather, for first century Jews like
St. John and the early Christians to whom he wrote, a lamb would
recall the sacrificial lambs offered in the Temple, especially on Passover. Jesus' appearing as "a lamb standing as though it had been
slain" (Rv 5:6) is intended to show how Jesus is the new Passover
lamb, sacrificed on Calvary. Just as the Passover lambs of old were
sacrificed to spare the first born Israelites in Egypt, so Jesus was
sacrificed on the cross to free all humanity from sin and death.

27 Rv 5:5-6.

Historical Context

This depth of interpretation cannot be gleaned, however, when one simply reads the text on a surface level and fails to weigh the author's intention. But how does one discern what the author's intention is? Again, the *Catechism* offers some helpful principles.

First, we must consider the text's historical context. As the *Catechism* explains, "In order to discover *the sacred authors' intention*, the reader must take into account the conditions of their time and culture."[28] Certain words or actions reported in the Bible may have a particular meaning in the original ancient culture. The more we factor in the historical context in which the text was written, the better we understand the author's intended message. But when we read texts completely divorced from their original context, we may make an erroneous interpretation.

For example, from a modern Western perspective, the Old Testament command "eye for an eye" (Ex 21:24; Lv 24:20; Dt 19:21) might seem like an exhortation to vengeance: if someone hurts you, you should hurt him back. However, when considered in the context of the ancient world—where individuals and tribes responded to injury by inflicting an even greater injury upon their enemies—this law makes a lot of sense. Far from promoting vengeance, "eye for an eye" is meant to prevent escalating violence and retribution by making legal punishments proportionate to the crimes committed.

Similarly, readers often miss the power of Jesus' first words to the apostles after he rose from the dead: "Peace to you!" (Lk 24:36). For some today, the word peace might denote absence of war. For others it may describe a balanced state of mind or "inner harmony." And for some young people, "peace" may merely mean, "Hey, how's it going?"

But in the first-century Jewish world, the word we translate as "peace"—*shalom*—denotes a rightly ordered relationship, covenant intimacy, and a relationship of trust. With this in mind, consider

---

[28] CCC 110.

the profound significance Christ's greeting would have had for the apostles as they encountered their Lord for the first time since they abandoned him on Good Friday. The apostles saw their Master and were "startled and frightened" (Lk 24:37)—probably because they feared he was coming in judgment upon them! However, instead of issuing condemnation, Jesus' first word to them was "peace." With this greeting, Jesus was not wishing them absence from war or inner harmony, and he certainly was not simply saying "hello" to them. Since the word "peace" described a rightly ordered relationship, Jesus was assuring them that he remained in full union with them even though they were disloyal. Despite their tragic cowardliness on Good Friday, Jesus still offered them friendship and forgiveness. He offered them *shalom*.

What Kind of Literature?

A second way to discern the human author's intention is to respect the literary genre he employs. The Bible uses a variety of literary forms. Historical narratives tell the story of God's plan of salvation in ancient Israel and the early Christian community (e.g., 1-2 Kings, the Gospels, Acts). In response to God's saving deeds, his people express praise and thanksgiving in poems or hymns that are scattered throughout the Bible (e.g., Ex 15; the Psalms; Rv 19:1-8). Laws such as those in Leviticus and Deuteronomy outline the structure and obligations for Israel's covenant relationship with God. Proverbial sayings reflect more customary principles for social interaction and for living life well (e.g., Proverbs and Ecclesiastes). Prophetic literature exhorts God's people to remain faithful to the law, calls them to repentance when they are unfaithful, and foretells how God will act in the future to bring judgment on the wicked and blessing on the faithful. Epistles—such as St. Paul's letters in the New Testament or Jeremiah's letter in Baruch 6—offer teaching, pastoral guidance, rebukes for disobedience, exhortations to faithfulness, and hope for the future in the form of a letter from an individual to another individual or group.

Keeping a work's literary genre in mind is helpful for interpreting any kind of literature. One should not read a chemistry textbook like a love letter or interpret a law from the Department of Motor Vehicles as a poetic text. (Imagine explaining to the police officer that you were just interpreting the speed limit metaphorically like a poem!)

The same is true with the Bible. We should not read a psalm as we do an historical narrative. When Psalm 23 says, "The Lord is my shepherd," we are not to conclude that the psalmist views God as an actual herder of sheep. As poetic prayers and hymns used for worship, the psalms typically use metaphor and other poetic devices. That is clearly the case here: God is like a shepherd in relation to his people, guiding them and protecting them from harm.

At the same time, when the gospels report that Jesus healed a blind man and rose from the dead, these accounts are not to be interpreted as mere allegories or metaphors having no roots in history. As historical narratives, the gospels are reporting what Jesus really taught and did.[29] Therefore, these accounts faithfully tell us that Jesus really did give sight to the blind and rise from the dead. In sum, we need to respect the literary genre used by the biblical writers. We should read laws legally, poems poetically, and history historically.

The Art of Biblical Narrative

A third way to discern the human author's intention is to take into account the modes of feeling, speaking, and narrating used in biblical times.[30] The way ancient peoples reported history, told stories, or wrote letters is often very different from the way we do so today. They did not always give straightforward, chronological,

---

[29] CCC 126.
[30] CCC 110.

"play-by-play" accounts of history but often organized material by themes and employed elaborate literary techniques that involved repetition, parallelism, allusion, and alliteration—artistry that modern readers sometimes miss.

For example, the rich theological points found in Genesis 1 are more deeply appreciated when we factor in the way the six days of creation unfold in the narrative. Numerous Scripture scholars have pointed out how the first three days correspond to the next three days of creation. On the first three days, God creates day and night (first day), sky and sea (second day), and land and vegetation (third day). Then on the fourth day, God creates the sun, moon, and stars to rule over the day and night, corresponding to what he created on the first day. On the fifth day, God creates the birds to fill the sky and the fish to fill the sea, corresponding to the second. And on the sixth day, God creates the beasts to crawl on the earth, corresponding to the land created on the third day.

Day 1:	Day & Night	←	Day 4:	Sun, Moon, & Stars
Day 2:	Sky & Sea	←	Day 5:	Birds & Fish
Day 3:	Land & Vegetation	←	Day 6:	The Beasts

Clearly, the author of Genesis 1 is setting up a series of parallels between the first three days of creation and the last three days to show how God is the divine architect, creating the universe with great order, first creating three realms on days 1-3 (time, space, and life) and then creating the rulers over those realms on days 4-6 (sun, moon, and stars over time; birds and fish filling sky and sea; and the beasts over the land where vegetation grows). Finally, God creates man and woman as the crowning of his creation, making them in his image and likeness and commissioning them to rule over all creation: "Let them have dominion over the fish of the sea, and over the birds of the air, and over the cattle, and over all the earth" (Gn 1:26).

All this is missed if we do not take into account the literary artistry of the biblical writers. The more we learn about the literary techniques and modes of narration used in biblical times, the better equipped we will be to discern the way the sacred writers shaped their accounts and the better able we will be to interpret the message they were intending to communicate.

CHAPTER 4

The Second Key: Be Attentive
to the Unity of Scripture

A s we have seen, understanding the human author's intention is an important first step in biblical interpretation. But since Scripture also has God as its author, there is a second vital principle for interpreting the Bible correctly: "Sacred Scripture must be read and interpreted in the light of the same Spirit by whom it was written."[31] This principle reminds us that the Bible is not merely a human document written long ago by people far removed from our lives. The Bible is God's timeless word to his people throughout history—a divine word originally spoken through human writers to a certain audience at a particular moment in time, but echoing through the centuries with profound implications for each new generation of Christians. Since the human writers of Scripture were inspired by the same Holy Spirit who continues to act in the Church and in our lives today, the Bible continues to be a personal word from God spoken to each new Christian. As Vatican II taught, "In the sacred books the Father who is in heaven comes to meet his children, and talks with them."[32]

---

[31] CCC 111, citing DV 12.
[32] DV 21.

So important is this second principle that Scripture would remain a dead letter without it.[33] Biblical interpretation that examines merely the intention of the human author, limiting its analysis to the meaning of the text in its original historical setting, locks the Bible in the past. Such an approach fails to see Scripture as a personal word, lovingly spoken to each individual soul. There are great dangers in viewing the Bible in such narrow terms. As Joseph Cardinal Ratzinger writes, "A mere historical reading of the Bible is not enough. We do not read it as the former words of humans; we read it as the word of God always present in a new way that was given to all ages through the people of a past age. To lodge this word solely in the past means to deny the Bible as the Bible."[34]

But practically, how does one read the Bible in this proper way? How does one read Scripture "in light of the same Spirit by whom it was written," so that the Bible can effectively speak to us today? The Second Vatican Council offers three criteria from the Catholic tradition for reading Scripture this way: 1) be attentive to the content and unity of the Bible; 2) read Scripture within the living Tradition of the Church; and 3) be attentive to the analogy of faith.[35]

Seeing the Whole

These three criteria from Vatican II represent the next three keys for interpreting Scripture. In this chapter, we will focus on one of these criteria, our second key for interpreting the Bible correctly: being attentive to "the content and unity of the whole Scripture."[36]

Behind the many different languages, authors, literary genres, and time periods in the Bible lies one unified story that starts at the beginning of time and continues to the present moment. The seventy-three diverse books of the Bible, each in its own particular

---

[33] See CCC 111.

[34] Joseph Cardinal Ratzinger, *A New Song for the Lord: Faith in Christ and the Liturgy Today* (New York: Crossroad, 1997), pp. 170-171.

[35] See DV 12; CCC 112-114.

[36] CCC 112.

way, together unfold the drama of God's plan of salvation, which has Jesus Christ's death and resurrection at the center. "Different as the books which comprise it may be, Scripture is a unity by reason of the unity of God's plan, of which Christ Jesus is the center and heart, open since his Passover."[37]

Thus, the Church, in this criterion for interpreting Scripture, exhorts us to read individual biblical verses and passages in light of the whole of Scripture. We should interpret the smaller pieces of the Bible as part of the larger story of salvation recorded in the Scriptures.

The Old and the New

This means we should be careful not to read biblical verses in isolation but in light of the whole of Scripture. Since the same Spirit inspired all the books of the Bible, the various books are mutually interpretive, shedding light on each other. It is thus that the Old and New Testaments are intimately united. One cannot fully appreciate the New Testament books apart from the Old Testament story which preceded them, and the Old Testament itself cannot be adequately understood without an eye to its fulfillment in the New. "As an old saying put it, the New Testament lies hidden in the Old and the Old Testament is unveiled in the New."[38]

Failing to consider the content and unity of the Bible leads to a deficient interpretation. Some Christians, for example, make the mistake of reading the New Testament without considering its Old Testament background. We should never approach the New Testament, for example, like a person who turns on the TV to catch the last three seconds of a football game. The home team is down by two points, and they attempt a field goal. If successful, of course, they will get three points and a victory, but if it is missed, they will lose. Even though the "last minute" fan has not seen the previous

---

[37] CCC 112.
[38] CCC 129.

59:57 of the game, he can jump in at the very end and completely understand the significance of a field goal attempt, fully entering into the drama of the game.

We might be able to do that with sports, but we cannot do that with the Bible. The New Testament, after all, is not like the last few seconds of a sporting event. The New Testament is more like the last chapter of a great book or the final scene of a thrilling movie. One must know the drama that went before in order to appreciate the climax of most stories.

Don't Fast-Forward

Imagine someone who hasn't seen the first or second films in *The Lord of the Rings* trilogy, *Fellowship of the Ring* and *The Two Towers*. Nonetheless, he rents the third film, *The Return of the King*, fast-forwarding to the end, to a scene in which a slimy creature jumps around and cries out in a creepy voice, "My precious!" just before he falls off a cliff into volcanic lava, carrying a gold ring with him.

Will such a viewer truly grasp the profound meaning of this climactic moment in *The Lord of the Rings* trilogy without knowing the plot, characters, and many twists and turns leading up to this point in the story? Certainly not. And yet, many Christians fast-forward through much of the Old Testament, thinking that they can jump right into the New Testament and understand the story without missing a beat. But readers who do not know the context of salvation history that precedes the coming of Christ—namely, the drama of God's interaction with his people Israel in the Old Testament—will not be able to grasp fully the meaning of Christ's life as the climax of that story. Being attentive to the content and unity of Scripture helps us to keep the "big picture" of the Bible in mind and to read the Old and New Testaments as a unified story. Such a perspective will always enrich our interpretation of the Bible.

Avoid Myopic Reading

Another way in which readers sometimes fail to consider the content and unity of the Bible is to interpret individual verses in isolation—apart from the wider context of the particular book and other books of the Bible. Since all of Scripture has the same divine author, other sections of Scripture shed important light on particular verses, passages, and scenes. Failing to read these verses in light of the whole limits one's ability to mine the Bible for all its worth. Let us consider an example that illustrates both the richness of interpreting the Bible with its content and unity in mind and the dangers of a myopic reading of Scripture that fails to do so.

How should we understand Jesus' addressing his mother as "woman" at the wedding of Cana?   After Mary asks Jesus to do something about the embarrassing wine shortage at this wedding feast, Jesus responds to her, saying: "O woman, what have you to do with me? My hour has not yet come" (Jn 2:4).

When this verse is read at face value, in isolation from the rest of the Bible, it seems like Jesus is pushing his mother away. To modern ears, someone calling his mother "woman" almost sounds like the words of a rebellious teenager! Thus, based on this verse alone, some readers might conclude that Jesus is rebuking his mother or distancing himself from her.

However, if we begin to apply the criterion about the content and unity of Scripture, we will see this is far from the case. First, when Jesus' words are read in light of the verses that immediately follow, we see clearly that Jesus is in no way pushing his mother away. Notice Mary's response to Jesus' words in the next verse. She says to the servants at the feast, "Do whatever he tells you" (Jn 2:5). Does Mary interpret Jesus' words as somehow negative or hurtful? Just the opposite. She seems to interpret Jesus' words as something positive. She assumes Jesus will fulfill her request and thus asks the servants to assist him. Jesus' own actions also suggest that his words are not meant to be understood as some harsh rebuke or rejection of his mother's request, for he responds to Mary's request positively by changing the water into wine. Thus, when Jesus' initial words in John 2:4 are read not in isolation but in light of the subsequent verses, it becomes clear that—whatever these cryptic words may mean—they were not something harsh or negative.

Second, if we interpret Jesus' words in light of the wider context of John's gospel, we discover that Jesus—far from pushing his mother way—is actually bestowing on Mary an exalted title that highlights her crucial role in God's plan of salvation. Consider how John's gospel starts with the words "In the beginning" (Jn 1:1), which harkens back to Genesis 1:1: "In the beginning God created the heavens and the earth." In the next four verses, John goes on to write of light, life, creation, and light shining in darkness—more images taken right out of the creation story (Jn 1:2-5; Gn 1:1-26). Thus John introduces the story of Jesus against the backdrop of the story of creation, highlighting how Jesus comes to bring about a renewal of all creation.

John's gospel continues this creation theme by setting up a series of days that establishes a new seven-day creation week. The sequence begins in 1:19 with the first episode in John's gospel. John then demarcates a second day in 1:29 with the words "the next day." He then uses the same phrase to note the third and fourth days in 1:35 and 1:43, respectively. Finally, after the succession of these first four days, the story of the wedding at Cana is introduced as taking place three days after the fourth day: "On the third day there was a marriage at Cana" (2:1). The third day after the fourth day would represent the seventh day in the gospel of John. These seven days at the beginning of John's gospel recall the seven days of the creation story in Genesis 1. Consequently, the wedding at Cana, coming on the seventh day, represents the climax of the new creation week in the gospel of John.

Now we are ready to understand the profound meaning of Jesus calling his mother "woman" at the wedding feast of Cana. Highlighting how this scene takes place on the seventh day of the new creation week, John's gospel leads us to view Jesus and Mary in light of the creation story. And in this context, Jesus calls Mary "woman." With the Genesis themes in the background, this title would bring to mind the famous "woman" of Genesis, Eve (Gn 2:23; 3:20)—the woman who played an important part in the first prophecy given to humanity. After the Fall, God confronted the serpent (the devil) and announced his eventual defeat, saying: "I will put enmity between you and the woman, and between your seed and her seed; he shall bruise your head, and you shall bruise his heel" (Gn 3:15).

These words, known as the *Protoevangelium* ("first gospel"), foretell how the woman one day will have a seed (a son) who will crush the head of the serpent.[39] Many centuries later, at the wedding feast of Cana, this prophecy begins to be fulfilled. By calling Mary "woman" with the creation story in the background, Jesus honors her in a way no woman ever had been honored before. She is the new Eve, the woman whose long-awaited son will defeat the devil and fulfill the prophecy of Genesis.

Here we see how the criterion about the content and unity of the Bible can make or break our interpretation of Scripture. When "Woman ..." in John 2:4 is read in light of the unity of Scripture, we can glimpse the heights of the Bible's revelation about Mary's role in God's saving plan: she is the new Eve. However, when we fail to consider the unity of Scripture, Jesus' words are seen in a myopic way. The broad horizons of salvation history do not come into view, and we are left with a fuzzy perspective on Jesus' words to his mother. We might even wrongly conclude that Jesus is rebuking Mary and distancing himself from her.

---

[39] CCC 410.

CHAPTER 5

The Third Key: Read Scripture within the Living Tradition of the Church

Have you ever found the Bible difficult to understand? The eighth chapter of the Acts of the Apostles tells the story of an Ethiopian man who struggled to comprehend the meaning of a certain prophecy from Isaiah. This man was a sincere believer in the God of Israel, traveling home after worshiping in the Temple, but he could not grasp the meaning of the Scriptures on his own.

Just at that moment, the Holy Spirit sent Philip to meet this traveling Ethiopian. Philip asked him, "Do you understand what you are reading?" And the Ethiopian replied, "How can I, unless some one guides me?" (Acts 8:30-31). Philip joined him in his chariot, told him the Good News of Jesus Christ, and explained how Jesus was the fulfillment of the prophecy he was reading. As a result of Philip's explanation, the Ethiopian came to understand the meaning of the Scriptures and asked to be baptized into the Christian faith.[40]

This story exemplifies one of the difficulties we face when the Bible is read in isolation from the community of believers. The Bible is meant to be read in the context of "the living Tradition of

---

[40] For more on Philip's role in Acts 8 as an analogy for Tradition, see Tim Gray, "Reading Scripture from the Inside-Out," *Lay Witness* (April 2001).

the whole Church."[41] If we try to read the Bible on our own, apart from the tradition that gave birth to the Scriptures, we will fail to understand its meaning. Like the Ethiopian, we need a guide.

In this chapter, we will consider a third key for interpreting the Bible: reading Scripture within the living Tradition of the Church. Sacred Tradition serves as a guide for making Scripture better understood and more active in the life of the Church. But what exactly is Tradition? Where do we find it? Why do we even need it? These are some of the topics we will explore in this chapter on the mystery of Sacred Tradition and the indispensable role it has in helping us understand the Bible and live according to it.

Jewish Discipleship

Ancient Jewish discipleship entailed much more than memorizing the oral teachings of the master. Jewish rabbis taught their students primarily not through spoken lessons or written texts but by their life example. Discipleship ultimately meant imitating the master. A disciple was invited to share in the rabbi's life and to learn from it.

Like other Jewish rabbis, Jesus also gathered disciples and invited a group of people to share in his life. He didn't say, "Come hear my lecture on the beatitudes," but "Come, follow me." Christ's disciples, therefore, were not students in the modern sense of those who merely attend a teacher's classes. They "followed" him from village to village throughout his public ministry, living with him, sharing meals with him, and praying with him. They watched the way he cared for the poor, helped the sick, and showed mercy to sinners. Day after day, Jesus' disciples witnessed the way he prayed to the Father, taught the crowds in his sermons, and called the people to repentance. They observed the way he instituted the Eucharist, forgave his enemies, and died for their sins. As disciples, they would have assimilated Christ's whole way of life. As a result,

---

[41] CCC 113.

when it came time for their own apostolic missions, they passed on not just ideas about God—doctrines to believe and moral principles to follow—but an entire way of life. It is this living transmission of the whole Christian reality that is at the heart of Sacred Tradition.

What Tradition Hands On

The *Catechism* makes this point when discussing the *content* of what the apostles passed on through Tradition. First, the apostles handed on to others what they themselves received directly from Christ—not just what they heard "from the lips of Christ," but also "his way of life and his works."[42] In other words, Tradition involves more than Christ's verbal teachings. It also involves the lived experiences and practices associated with his ministry. It includes "everything which contributes toward the holiness of life and increase in faith of the people of God."[43]

Second, the apostles also handed on what they learned about Christ "at the prompting of the Holy Spirit."[44] Jesus promised the apostles he would give them the Holy Spirit, who would "teach you all things, and bring to your remembrance all that I have said to you" (Jn 14:26). Even after Jesus ascended into heaven, the Holy Spirit continued to guide the apostles throughout their lives in an ever deeper understanding of his teachings.

The *Catechism* also explains *how* this Tradition was passed on to others. The apostles handed on this Tradition to their followers in three principal ways: 1) "by the spoken word of their preaching," 2) "by the example they gave," and 3) "by the institutions they established."[45] We see each of these three modes of Tradition in the book of Acts, for example. The apostles (and their successors) pass on this tradition by *preaching* the Gospel of Christ (Acts 2:14-36, 3:11-26, 5:42, 7:1-53, 10:34-43). They invite others to follow

---

[42]   CCC 76, citing DV 7.
[43]   DV 8.
[44]   CCC 76, citing DV 7.
[45]   Ibid.

their *example*, living in community with them, praying with them, serving those in need, and participating in their mission (2:42-47, 4:23-37, 6:1-6). Finally, the apostles established various *institutions* that concretely embodied what they received from Christ, including baptism (2:38-41, 8:38, 10:48, 16:15), the Eucharist (2:42, 20:7), a council (15:2-29), and presbyters who participated in their mission (15:4, 6, 23; 20:17, 28-29).

As we can see, the apostles immediately began fulfilling Christ's Great Commission to make disciples of all nations, baptizing them and teaching all Christ had taught them (Mt 28:18-20). Long before the New Testament was written, the apostles were already handing on the Christian faith to others through their preaching, baptizing, and welcoming of converts into the Christian life. They did not wait for the New Testament canon of Scripture to develop, but began bringing others into communion with Christ through their preaching and example, and through the institutions they established—in other words, through Sacred Tradition.

Where Do We Find Tradition Today?

This living transmission of the faith from the apostolic age to the present is accomplished through the Holy Spirit in the Church. As the *Catechism* explains, "Through Tradition, 'the Church, in her doctrine, life, and worship perpetuates and transmits to every generation all that she herself is, all that she believes.' 'The sayings of the holy Fathers are a witness to the life-giving presence of this Tradition.'" [46] Here, the *Catechism* identifies at least four key "places" where we can come in contact with Sacred Tradition:

1. The Church's **doctrine:** As taught in the early Christian creeds, the *Catechism*, Church councils, and other magisterial teachings, as well as the writings of the Doctors

---

[46] CCC 78, citing DV 8.

of the Church who are officially recognized in Catholicism as model teachers of the Catholic faith.

2. The Church's **life:** For example, the lives of the saints, religious movements, popular devotions, and common practices that have gained acceptance in the Church.

3. The Church's **worship:** The Church's liturgy, feasts, and sacraments; also, sacred music and art that expresses the Church's worship of God.

4. The **Church Fathers:** Early Church leaders and theologians, such as Sts. Ignatius of Antioch, John Chrysostom, Basil, Jerome, and Augustine. They are principal witnesses to the Church's living Tradition, not only because of their closeness to the apostolic era, but also because of how their writings systematized, deepened, and greatly shaped the Church's understanding of the apostolic Tradition.

In sum, the Church's doctrine, life, and worship, along with the writings of the Church Fathers, stand as bearers of the apostolic Tradition. They help bridge the almost two-thousand-year gap between Christ's followers today and his original disciples in Galilee. The more we read the Scriptures in light of Tradition, the more we become united to the Christians who have gone before us. In fact, when we read Scripture with Tradition, we become like the Ethiopian man who was enlightened by Philip. We have a living guide to make the Scriptures "more powerfully understood" and active in us.[47] In Sacred Tradition, "God, who spoke of old, uninterruptedly converses with the bride of his beloved Son, and the Holy Spirit, through whom the living voice of the Gospel resounds in the Church and, through her, in the world, leads unto all truth those who believe and makes the word of Christ dwell abundantly in them (see Col 3:16)."[48]

---

[47] DV 8.
[48] Ibid.

Does Tradition Develop?

While we can speak about the "development" of Tradition, this does not mean the *content* of what is handed on from the apostles changes or grows, but simply that the Church's *understanding* of that content deepens. Guided by the Holy Spirit, the Church, through the contemplation and study of believers and the preaching of the apostles' successors (the bishops in union with the pope), arrives at an ever more mature understanding of the mysteries of faith and their application for the particular needs of each new generation of Christians.

But not all developing practices in the Church are a part of Sacred Tradition. As we have seen, Sacred Tradition refers to that which the apostles received from Jesus' teaching and example or from what they learned from the Holy Spirit and then handed on to others. We refer to this as Tradition with a capital "T" in order to distinguish it from "various theological, disciplinary, liturgical, or devotional traditions, born in the local churches over time."[49] These latter are called "ecclesial traditions" (with a lowercase "t"). Unlike Sacred Tradition, which is of divine origin and whose purpose is the handing on of the Christian faith from one generation to the next, ecclesial traditions arise in different places and times, are adapted to local cultures, and may be "modified or even abandoned under the guidance of the Church's [M]agisterium."[50] Thus, for example, the necessity of baptism and the Eucharist in the Christian life is part of Sacred Tradition, a belief proclaimed by the Church from its very beginning. Some of the particular prayers and rituals associated with baptism and the Mass, however, have been shaped by local customs and the needs of a particular church. The traditions (lowercase "t") connected with these sacraments, therefore, may vary depending on the culture and time period in which they arose, and they may evolve in the future.

[49] CCC 83.
[50] Ibid.

So the Bible Isn't the Only Way to Know God's Revelation?

As we have seen, Catholics, unlike most Protestant Christians, do not believe that the Bible is the only source of divine revelation. (For that matter, neither do Eastern Orthodox Christians.) This is not something Scripture teaches, nor is it rooted in traditional Christian practice throughout the centuries. Ironically, the notion of *sola scriptura*—i.e., that the Bible is the only infallible authority for Christian faith—is itself unbiblical, unhistorical, and unworkable.

In the first place, *sola scriptura* is an *unbiblical* belief. Nowhere does Scripture say that it is the exclusive source of divine authority. In fact, the Bible itself teaches that we must hold on not only to what was written down, but to the oral traditions of the apostles as well: "So then, brethren, stand firm and hold to the traditions which you were taught by us, either by word of mouth or by letter" (2 Thess 2:15). Here, St. Paul does not simply approve of oral tradition, but he *commands* the Thessalonians—and, by extension, all Christians—to follow it. Rejecting oral tradition is thus unbiblical. In another passage, St. Paul assumes the presence of oral tradition among the Ephesians when he exhorts them to remember "the words of the Lord Jesus, how he said, 'It is more blessed to give than to receive'" (Acts 20:35)—a statement of Christ nowhere found in the gospels or any other book of the Bible, but one that Paul assumes is well known by the Ephesians. Since this quote from Christ is not found anywhere in Scripture, the only way the Ephesians could know Jesus said this is through oral tradition. Moreover, when the Bible discusses "the pillar and bulwark of the truth," it does so not in reference to Scripture but to the Church (1 Tm 3:15).

Second, *sola scriptura* is *unhistorical*. For the first 1,400 years of Christianity, faithful Christians read Scripture in the context of the Church's teachings and Sacred Tradition. The very notion of *sola scriptura* would have been foreign to the earliest Christians. It is a man-made tradition without foundation in ancient Christian practice.

Third, *sola scriptura* is *unworkable*. The Scriptures are intended to be read in the heart of the Church and in union with the Church's Tradition. They cannot be properly understood divorced from the community of believers and cut off from Sacred Tradition. An individualistic approach to the Bible that says, "I don't need the Church or Tradition; God will show me the meaning his word," will only lead to greater division within Christianity. In fact, since Martin Luther adopted the idea of *sola scriptura* in the sixteenth century, there have been thousands of divisions sown in the Body of Christ as various rival Christian groups claim that the Holy Spirit is guiding them to the right interpretation of Scripture. According to the *World Christian Encyclopedia*, there are currently more than 33,000 different Christian denominations. This is largely the fruit of the individualistic approach to Scripture fostered by *sola scriptura*. Wrenching the Scriptures out of their home—the Church—can only lead to greater divisions among Christians.

CHAPTER 6

The Fourth Key: Read Scripture within the Symphony of God's Revelation

Like three leading instruments in God's "symphony," Scripture, Tradition, and the Magisterium play distinctive roles in God's plan of revealing himself to his people. Each contributes in a particular way to making God's revelation known, working in harmony with the other two. As Vatican II taught, "It is clear, therefore, that Sacred Tradition, Sacred Scripture, and the teaching authority of the Church, in accord with God's most wise design, are so linked and joined together that one cannot stand without the others, and that all together and each in its own way under the action of the one Holy Spirit contribute effectively to the salvation of souls."[51]

This beautiful harmony between Scripture, Tradition, and the Magisterium lies at the center of our fourth key for interpreting the Bible: being "attentive to the analogy of faith."[52] An analogy is a set of similarities between two or more things. The analogy of faith refers to the harmonious agreement between all the truths of the faith revealed by God and entrusted to the Church: the truths written in Scripture and the truths handed on through Sacred

---

[51] DV 10.
[52] CCC 114.

Tradition. Both Scripture and Tradition flow from the same divine source. Therefore, since God is the source of all revealed truth, Scripture can never contradict the elements of Christian faith such as the Creed or Church teaching, and similarly, the Christian faith itself can never be at odds with Scripture. In sum, the analogy of faith is "the coherence of the truths of faith among themselves and within the whole plan of Revelation."[53]

Reading "In Tune"

This principle helps ensure that one's interpretation of Scripture remains on the right track. Truth cannot contradict truth. Therefore, since there is a unity of truth in God's revelation, one's interpretation of Scripture must be in harmony with Sacred Tradition and the teachings of the Church. If one were to interpret a passage of the Bible in a way that was opposed to Church teaching, that would be a sure sign that this understanding was "out of tune" with the symphony of God's revelation. In this way, being attentive to the analogy of faith guards our interpretation of Scripture, preventing us from falling into error. For example, if we were to interpret Jesus' institution of the Eucharist at the Last Supper in a purely figurative way—as referring not to the Real Presence of Jesus but merely to a symbolic reminder of him—our interpretation would be in contradiction with magisterial teaching on the Eucharist and out of step with the way this passage has been interpreted throughout the centuries by the Fathers, Doctors, and saints of the Church.

Furthermore, the analogy of faith not only serves as a check and balance on our interpretation of the Bible, preventing us from falling into error. It also guides our interpretation of Scripture, illuminating the deeper meaning of biblical texts. For example, the New Testament often refers to Jesus as the "Son of God," but the precise meaning of Christ's divine sonship is not spelled out

---

[53] CCC 114.

explicitly in the Bible. In fact, some early Christians interpreted this title in a metaphorical way, as referring to Jesus' closeness to God or to his being adopted by God as a Son—but not to his being truly divine. The Council of Nicea in AD 325 clarified the meaning of Jesus' divine sonship, explaining that Jesus is "of the same substance" as the Father. In other words, Jesus shares the same divine nature as the Father. This teaching is summed up in the Nicene Creed, which we recite at Mass. We do not say Jesus is "close to the Father" or is "an adopted son of the Father," but that he is *"one in being* with the Father." This authoritative teaching about Christ's divine sonship sheds important light on the many New Testament passages that refer to Jesus as God's Son. This teaching not only prevents us from viewing Jesus as a merely human son adopted by God but also invites us to contemplate Christ's divinity and the profound union he has with the Father.

The Only Authentic Interpreter?

Some may wonder, though, how the Catholic Church can claim that its Magisterium is the only authentic interpreter of Scripture. Where do the Church's popes and bishops get the authority to teach officially for God's people? Does the Bible say anything about this?

Both the New Testament and the writings of the Church Fathers make it clear that Christ gave his authority to the apostles and their successors to teach and lead the Church.

First, the New Testament highlights that Jesus chose twelve apostles and gave them authority to teach, heal, and act in his name. "And he called the Twelve together and gave them power and authority over all demons and to cure diseases, and he sent them out to preach the kingdom of God and to heal" (Lk 9:1-2). After his resurrection, Jesus entrusted to the apostles the same mission he had received from his heavenly Father: "As the Father has sent me, even so I send you" (Jn 20:21). Before ascending into heaven, Jesus gave the apostles authority to baptize, teach, and

make disciples of all nations, and promised that he would always be
with them in this mission (see Mt 28:18-20). Here, we see that the
apostles were not simply important Church leaders who should be
respected and followed. They were "ministers of a new covenant"
(2 Cor 3:6), "ambassadors for Christ" (2 Cor 5:20), and "servants
of Christ and stewards of the mysteries of God" (1 Cor 4:1). In this
sense, the apostles represented Jesus Christ and taught in his name.
Jesus made a close identification between his teachings and those
of his apostles: "He who hears you hears me, and he who rejects
you rejects me, and he who rejects me rejects him who sent me"
(Lk 10:16). In other words, listening to the apostles is listening
to Christ. No one in the first century could say to Jesus, "I want
to follow you and your teachings, but I don't want to accept the
apostles' teachings." To reject the teachings of the apostles is to
reject Jesus Christ himself.

Apostolic Succession

Second, the apostles passed on this authority to other men who
would carry out Christ's mission. Like the apostles themselves,
these successors (i.e., the bishops) do not take the place of Christ
but represent him. They teach not on their own authority but with
the authority of Christ himself. The importance of the apostles'
successors, the bishops, was already well known in the first
decades of the Church. St. Paul writes about the office of bishop
(1 Tm 3:1-7), noting that a bishop must hold firm to the Gospel
that has been passed on to him because he has the special role of
faithfully teaching the "sound doctrine" he received, guarding it
against skewed interpretations and attacks from those who oppose
it (see Ti 1:7-9). Then, in the first generation of Christians after
the apostles, St. Clement of Rome clearly writes that the authority
Christ entrusted to the apostles had been given to the apostles'
successors, the bishops. In his letter to the Corinthians, written
around AD 96, Clement says the apostles "appointed their first

converts—after testing them by the Spirit—to be bishops and deacons for the believers of the future. This was in no way an innovation, for bishops and deacons had already been spoken of in Scripture long before that."[54] Similarly, another early Church father, St. Ignatius, bishop of Antioch, calls on Christians to follow the authority of the bishops as if they were following Christ himself. In a letter from about AD 107, Ignatius warns the Christians in Tralles to obey their bishop as if he were Christ and "never [to] act independently of the bishop."[55] He develops this theme even more in his letter to the Christians in Smyrna, which says: "Follow your bishop, every one of you, as obediently as Jesus Christ followed the Father. Obey your clergy too, as you would the Apostles ... Make sure that no step affecting the church is ever taken by anyone without the bishop's sanction ... Where the bishop is seen, there let all his people be; just as wherever Jesus is present, we have the catholic Church."[56]

The earliest Christians saw the need to follow the leadership and teaching authority of the bishops. As the successors of the apostles, they were seen as authoritative interpreters of God's word. Following the authority of the bishops in the early Church would have been crucial just to read the Bible, for (as we will see) it was they who officially taught which of the many early Christian writings were actually part of the New Testament Scriptures. Therefore, without the authority of Jesus Christ entrusted to the Catholic Church, we would not even have known for sure which books were inspired by God and therefore part of the Bible.

---

[54] St. Clement of Rome, *First Epistle to the Corinthians*, 42, in *Early Christian Writings*, trans. by Maxwell Staniforth (London: Penguin Books, 1987).

[55] St. Ignatius of Antioch, *Epistle to the Trallians*, 2, in *Early Christian Writings*.

[56] St. Ignatius of Antioch, *Epistle to the Smyrnaeans*, 8, in *Early Christian Writings*.

Chapter 7

The Fifth Key: Use the Four Senses of Scripture

The four senses of Scripture provide us with our fifth interpretive key for unlocking many spiritual treasures in the Bible.[57] This key can help us draw vital connections between the Old and New Testaments, the Catholic faith, and our own spiritual lives. With this approach, the people, places, and events of the Bible go from being distant realities, far removed from our day-to-day experience, to being relevant to our own lives and serving as models for us pilgrims on the Christian path.

Traditionally, there are four senses of Scripture, which are outlined in the *Catechism*, nos. 115-119:

Literal Sense: "[T]he meaning conveyed by the words of Scripture." The actual person, event, place, or thing described in the biblical text. The literal sense gives rise to the following three "spiritual senses."

Allegorical Sense: How those persons, events, places, or things in the literal sense point to Christ and his work of redemption.

Moral Sense: How the literal sense points to the Christian's life in the Church.

---

[57] This chapter is based on my article, "Making Sense Out of Scripture," *Lay Witness* (October 1996), pp. 6-7, 27.

Anagogical Sense: How the literal sense points to the Christian's heavenly destiny and the last things.

The foundation for the four senses of Scripture is God's unique way of communicating. Humans communicate primarily through words and actions. However, God communicates not only through his words and deeds,[58] but also through the very things he has created. As St. Thomas Aquinas explains, "That God is the author of Holy Scripture should be acknowledged, and he has the power not only of adapting words to signify things (which human writers can also do), but also of *adapting things themselves* [to signify other things]."[59]

In other words, God not only communicates through the words of Scripture, but, since he is the Creator and the Lord of history, he gives special meaning to the things, people, and events mentioned in Scripture and uses them as signs to tell us something about his plan of salvation. This may occur even without the human author's awareness, since God is co-author of Scripture.

The Four Temples

A classic example to demonstrate the four senses is the Temple. In the literal sense, the Temple was the actual building that once stood in Jerusalem, in which the Israelite priests offered sacrifice, the people worshiped, and God dwelt in the Holy of Holies.

But this Temple of the Old Testament has even more importance because God has used it to tell us about greater realities in the New Testament—Jesus and the Christian life. *Allegorically*, the Temple points to Jesus, who said he was the true temple which would be destroyed and raised up in three days (Jn 2:19-21). Just as the Temple in Jerusalem was the place of sacrifice for the Jews, so does Jesus' body house the perfect sacrifice on Calvary for all humanity.

The moral sense of the Temple is found in the Christian, whose

---

[58] CCC 53.
[59] St. Thomas Aquinas, *Summa Theologiae*, I, 1, 10 (emphasis added).

body is "a temple of the Holy Spirit" (1 Cor 6:19). Just as the Temple contained the awesome presence of God, so the bodies of Christians hold the presence of the Holy Spirit by virtue of their baptism. Anagogically, the Jerusalem Temple finds its eschatological meaning in the heavenly sanctuary, where God will dwell among us in our eternal home, as described in the book of Revelation (e.g., Rv 21:22).

Sometimes associated with terms such as spiritual exegesis, typology, or *sensus plenior*, this method of interpreting Scripture is rooted in Catholic Tradition and has been used by many great saints, Doctors, and Fathers of the Church, and even by Jesus and the New Testament writers themselves. The *Catechism*, the Pontifical Biblical Commission, and Pope Benedict XVI have encouraged the use of this traditional approach to Scripture.

How Jesus Interpreted Scripture

Jesus himself viewed people and things in the Old Testament as signs that point to him and shed light on his mission. For example, Jesus refers to the Old Testament account of Jonah and the whale as prefiguring his own death and resurrection: "For as Jonah was three days and three nights in the belly of the whale, so will the Son of man be three days and three nights in the heart of the earth ... behold, something greater than Jonah is here" (Mt 12:40-41).

Similarly, the New Testament writers understood how God uses things, people, and events of the Old Testament to tell us something about his saving plan. For example, St. Paul describes Adam as a "type" of Christ (Rom 5:14), a sign telling us about Jesus: "For as by one man's disobedience many were made sinners, so by one man's obedience many will be made righteous" (Rom 5:19). Indeed, Jesus is the new Adam, the father of a new humanity in grace, righteousness, and life (see Rom 5:15-19).

Here are a few other examples: St. Peter views Noah's Ark, which saved people during the waters of the flood, as shedding light on the sacrament of baptism, which now saves Christians by our passing through the waters of the new covenant (1 Pt 3:20-21). Hebrews describes Israel's tabernacle, high priest, and sacrifices as "a copy and shadow of the heavenly sanctuary" (Heb 8:5). First Corinthians emphasizes how Israel's experiences of trials and failures in the desert were recorded in Exodus not for mere historical record, but to tell us something about the Christian life: "Now these things happened to them as a warning, but they were written down for our instruction" (1 Cor 10:11).

The Church Fathers read the Scriptures in this way, with the firm belief that, since the Bible contains God's inspired word, everything in it must have some significance for readers of every age. One of the most common themes found in the Fathers' practice of spiritual exegesis is the relationship between the Exodus and Christian baptism. Just as the Israelites escaped from slavery in Egypt, passed through the waters of the Red Sea, and headed toward the Promised Land, so are Christians freed from the spiritual bondage of sin and death by passing through the waters of baptism to begin their journey to the ultimate Promised Land, their heavenly home with Jesus.

St. Cyril of Jerusalem, in his instruction to early Church catechumens (i.e., those preparing for baptism), beautifully elaborates on this theme:

> You just know that the symbol of Baptism is found in ancient history ... There [in Exodus] we have Moses sent by God into Egypt; here [in Baptism] we have Christ sent by the Father into the world; there is need to free the oppressed people from Egypt, here to rescue men tyrannized over sin in this world; there the blood of the lamb turns aside the Destroyer; here the Blood of the true Lamb, Jesus Christ, puts the demons to flight; there the tyrant pursues the people even into the sea; here the shameless and bold demon follows them even

> to the holy fountains; one tyrant is drowned in the sea,
> the other is destroyed in the water of salvation.[60]

Cultivating Orthodoxy

Referring to this traditional approach to interpreting Scripture, John Henry Cardinal Newman writes, "It may be almost laid down as an historical fact that the mystical interpretation and orthodoxy will stand or fall together."[61] Why would the four senses be so important to orthodox faith?

Discovering the connections between the Old Testament, Christ, and the Christian life shows the continuity in God's plan of salvation, allowing us to see more clearly that from the very beginning—from Adam and Abraham to Moses and the prophets—God has been preparing humanity for Jesus Christ and the Catholic Church. This is why studying the Old Testament is vitally important for understanding Jesus and the essence of the Catholic faith. Take, for example, the Old Covenant Passover lamb. In its literal sense, the paschal lamb was eaten by Israelite families as the central part of the annual Passover meal, which commemorated Israel's deliverance from slavery in Egypt. But the spiritual senses show how God used that lamb as a preparation for understanding Jesus on the cross as the new paschal sacrifice and for understanding the Eucharist as the true Passover meal of the New Covenant, through which God delivers us from the spiritual bondage of sin.

More than Metaphors

We need to recognize, however, that the connections between the Old and the New—between the past, present, and future—

---

[60] St. Cyril of Jerusalem, *PG*, 32, 1068 A, as quoted in J. Danielou, *The Bible and the Liturgy* (Notre Dame, IN: University of Notre Dame Press, 1956), p. 96.
[61] John Henry Cardinal Newman, *The Arians of the Fourth Century* (London: Longmans, Green and Co., 1890), p. 405.

are not arbitrary but are rooted in God's plan of salvation. In other words, the four senses of Scripture are no mere metaphorical associations. This method of interpretation is not a creative enterprise in which one looks for nice images from the Old Testament that can help explain the Catholic faith. Rather, spiritual exegesis uncovers the great unity in God's salvific plan as carried out in history. The Church Fathers, for example, didn't invent the connections between the Exodus and baptism. Instead, they perceived the connections that were rooted in Scripture and history. They perceived that God orchestrated the Exodus event not only to liberate Israel from Egypt, but also to serve as a sign prefiguring baptism. Similarly, St. John did not creatively devise connections between the Temple in Jerusalem and the temple of Christ's body. Rather, he saw that God gave the Temple in Jerusalem to prefigure Christ. As the *Catechism* explains, "Thanks to the unity of God's plan, not only the text of Scripture but also the realities and events about which it speaks can be signs."[62] Theologian Henri Cardinal De Lubac similarly affirms:

> [I]f, for example, the manna is really the figure of the
> Eucharist, or if the sacrifice of the Paschal Lamb really
> pre-figures the redemptive death, the reason for this
> is not extrinsic [related] to resemblance alone, no
> matter how striking this may be. There is actually an
> "inherent" continuity and "ontological bond" between
> the two facts, and this is due to the same divine will
> which is active in both situations and which from stage
> to stage is pursuing a single Design—the Design which
> is the real object of the Bible.[63]

---

[62] CCC 117.
[63] H. De Lubac, *The Sources of Revelation* (New York: Herder and Herder, 1968), p. 37.

You Can Use the Four Senses

No doubt, understanding the four senses of Scripture is bound to transform your reading of the Bible. By using this Catholic approach to Scripture, you can more easily overcome the distance of time and discover the intimate solidarity that exists between the people of God in the Bible and your life in the Catholic Church today.

When we keep the four senses in mind, the biblical narratives become much more than stories from the ancient past. Whether we are reading the accounts about Abraham, the Temple, or the Flood, these age-old stories are no longer far removed from our lives today. Instead, they are intimately bound up with the present. As we saw above, the Passover is not merely a Jewish feast; it has become the essential backdrop for understanding the Eucharist. Similarly, as many spiritual writers have shown, Israel's testing in the wilderness for forty years is a model for the trials and purifications in the "spiritual desert" or "dark night" of the Christian life. Finally, the baptismal liturgy proclaims how the waters of the Red Sea or the Jordan River not only were instruments of redemption for the Israelites under Moses and Joshua, but also serve as preparations for understanding the redemptive waters of baptism. All these examples point to the fact that the same God who was fathering the ancient Israelites continues to work in similar ways with his children today. By calling our attention to the profound connections between the biblical world and the Christian life, the four senses of Scripture ultimately should lead us to our knees—to a deeper level of praise and thanksgiving for God's magnificent story of salvation, which he continues to write in the fabric of history and in our very lives.

PART III

WHERE DID THE BIBLE COME FROM?

CHAPTER 8

The New Testament Canon and the Gnostic "Gospels"

While many Old Testament books were revered as Scripture by the early Church, the first generation of Christians began composing their own writings by the middle of the first century. Many of these writings, such as the letters of Paul and the four gospels, were copied and shared with other Christian communities, and they grew in use and esteem as Christianity spread throughout the world. Although there were many texts written by Christians and circulated in the first three centuries, the ones that were in harmony with the beliefs of the Christian faith and that proved to be, over time, the most useful for preaching, teaching, and worship gained the widest acceptance in the early Church.

We see a basic level of acceptance for many of the New Testament books already within the first two centuries of Christianity in the writings of the most respected Christian leaders of this period. Many of these bishops and theologians (known as the Church Fathers) either explicitly quoted from or alluded to ideas from the four gospels, the letters of Paul, and other writings that came to be part of the New Testament. Furthermore, in the late second and third centuries, the Church Fathers began clarifying which of the Christian texts they considered to be most authoritative, and they started developing lists of the official New Testament books.

By the fourth century, the collection of New Testament books became fixed with the same twenty-seven books we have in our Bibles today. In AD 367, St. Athanasius, the bishop of Alexandria, listed these twenty-seven books—and these alone—as the authoritative Christian writings that could be read at Mass. This same list of twenty-seven New Testament books was given by a wider group of bishops at two councils in the early Church, the Council of Hippo in AD 393 and the Council of Carthage in 397. And this twenty-seven-book list was reaffirmed in a definitive manner by the Council of Trent in the sixteenth century. Christians—Catholic and Protestant alike—revere these same twenty-seven books as being divinely inspired and part of the "canon" of Scripture.

Criteria for Acceptance

The twenty-seven books of the New Testament gained widespread acceptance in the early Church and were confirmed as being part of the inspired Scriptures for several reasons:

1. These books were rooted in the *apostolic tradition*. They were written either by one of the apostles themselves (e.g., Matthew and John) or by a disciple or coworker of an apostle (e.g., Mark was a disciple of Peter, and Luke was a coworker of Paul).

2. They were known for their *catholicity* (or "universality"). In other words, they had relevance not just for one particular community or region of the Church but were applicable to and revered by Christians throughout the world.

3. They were considered *orthodox*, meaning they were in harmony with the teachings of the apostles. No writing could be considered authoritative if it was not congruous with the Church's teaching, especially as it was summed up in the Creed. For example, a bishop in Antioch banned a

writing called the gospel of Peter from being used because it denied the humanity of Christ.

4. They were used in the *sacred liturgy*. They were used not only for spiritual reading and teaching, but also for divine worship in the Mass.

Gnostic "Gospels"?

In recent years, the popular media has drawn attention to a group of ancient writings known as the Gnostic gospels. Some writers claim that these Gnostic texts offer an alternative view of Christianity, one that is actually earlier and, thus, more authentic than the portrayal of the faith found in the canonical gospels of Matthew, Mark, Luke, and John. According to this view, the four canonical gospels were not the earliest gospels written. Originally, there were a variety of gospels that offered diverse views about Jesus, Christian morality, and spirituality. According to these scholars, it was only in later centuries that Church leaders began suppressing these texts and favoring the four canonical gospels.

Now that modern archaeology has discovered these Gnostic gospels, they argue that Christianity needs a total makeover. In their view, the new insights these Gnostic texts offer challenge traditional beliefs about Jesus and demonstrate that Christians have been seriously mistaken about the "historical" Jesus. Thus Christianity needs to be revised according to their new "insights."

However, the existence of these Gnostic writings should not be headline news. They had already been widely known for many centuries through the writings of Church Fathers such as Irenaeus, Hippolytus, and Tertullian. In addition, portions of some of the original Gnostic manuscripts were discovered between 1880 and 1920, culminating in the most significant discovery in 1945 of a collection of ancient scrolls near the town of Nag Hammadi in Egypt. These scrolls comprise more than fifty texts and represent the largest and most important collection of Gnostic writings.

Gnosticism

What exactly was Gnosticism? Simply put, Gnosticism was a religious-philosophical movement of thought that viewed the physical world as evil and the spiritual world as good. To the Gnostic, salvation is found in the soul's escape from the body and the physical world. At least some of the Gnostic writings contain many beliefs that are not found in the first century of Christianity, including the following: the creator of the world is evil; the rejection of the Old Testament God; Jesus did not have an actual physical body; Jesus did not die on the cross, only his "body substitute"; women are not worthy of life. It is easy to see why these gospels never gained widespread acceptance in the early Church: they were directly opposed to orthodox Christian beliefs. There is no reference supporting these ideas in first- and early second-century Christian writings, and there never was a time when the Christian Church recognized these "gospels" as expressions of authentic Christianity.

Scholars hold that most of the Nag Hammadi documents are copies of texts originally written in the second and third centuries, later than the writing of the New Testament texts. Nearly all scholars—Christian and non-Christian alike—agree that the New Testament itself was written within the first century, with some of Paul's letters being written as early as about AD 50. Thus the Nag Hammadi scrolls certainly are not the earliest Christian records since they come generations after the writings of Paul and the gospels.

Within a hundred years after the death of the last apostle, the Church already recognized the gospels of Matthew, Mark, Luke, and John as authoritative Scripture and part of the developing New Testament canon. For example, around AD 125, an early Church bishop named Papias wrote about how the words and deeds of Jesus were passed on from the apostles to him; he mentions three of the New Testament gospels (Matthew, Mark, and John)—but not any of the Gnostic gospels. Similarly, when Tatian compiled the different gospel accounts into one harmonized text in AD 170, he synthesized Matthew, Mark, Luke, and John—but not any of the Gnostic gospels. By the end of the second century, the fourfold Gospel was largely fixed in the Christian tradition, so much so that Irenaeus in AD 177 could write:

> As there are four quarters of the world in which we live, and four universal winds, and as the church is dispersed over all the earth, and the Gospel is the pillar and base of the church, so it is natural that it should have four pillars, breathing immortality from every quarter and kindling human life anew. Clearly therefore the Word ... having been made manifest to the human race, has given us the gospel in fourfold form, but held together by one Spirit.[64]

Since the Gnostic gospels were written one hundred to three hundred years after Jesus' earthly life, they do not give us any "revolutionary" historical insights into the "real" Jesus. Texts from this later time period might provide some interesting insights into the intellectual and social climate of certain Gnostic sects, but they are not going to give us much reliable historical information about the life of Jesus Christ. In fact, most of these Gnostic documents are as far removed from the world of Jesus as we are today from the worlds of Abraham Lincoln and George Washington. In contrast, the four original gospels were composed within only a few decades after Christ, when many eyewitnesses to his words and deeds were still alive. Certainly, accounts from the first generation of Christianity are bound to give us a lot more historical evidence about Jesus than accounts from Gnostic-like fringe groups that appeared several generations after his lifetime.

---

[64] St. Ireneaus, *Against the Heresies*, III.

Reliability of Manuscript Tradition

Some may wonder whether the original books of the New Testament were copied and passed on to us today in a reliable way. After all, there were no printing presses or photocopiers in the ancient world to ensure that the copying process was free of errors or willful revisions. So how do we know that the set of New Testament books found in our Bibles is an accurate representation of the original New Testament?

The New Testament we have today is not only trustworthy; its books are by far the most reliable texts we have from the ancient world. The sheer number of ancient manuscript copies of the New Testament books is impressive. And some of these copies are ancient, very close to when the original manuscripts were composed.

To better illustrate this point, let's compare the New Testament manuscript tradition to the second best attested work in antiquity: the *Iliad*, the ancient Greek epic by Homer. Homer composed the *Iliad* around 800 BC, but we have no original manuscript of the work. Our modern editions of this classical work are based on manuscripts found long after Homer's lifetime. Of the approximately 650 extant manuscripts of the *Iliad*, the oldest dates from around AD 200 to 300—about 1,000 years after Homer's death! Nevertheless, most scholars agree that these very late copies of the *Iliad* are reliable representations of Homer's original work—even though they date from more than a millennium after its composition.

Let's now turn our attention to the New Testament. In comparison to the *Iliad*, the New Testament has a much stronger manuscript tradition. There are many more ancient manuscripts of the New Testament (about 5,000 of at least part of the New Testament), and these manuscripts are much closer in date to the originals. The New Testament was written within the first century, and we have copies of some of those New Testament writings from within just a few decades after they were composed.

We have fragments and major portions of individual New Testament books dating from the second and third centuries, and bound copies of the entire New Testament date from the fourth and fifth centuries. So there is only a two- to three-hundred-year gap between the copies and their original manuscripts. In contrast, there is a thousand-year gap between Homer and the earliest extant copies of the *Iliad*, which is considered a very reliable work. Therefore, the New Testament has a much stronger manuscript history than any other writing in the ancient world.

But how do we know these New Testament manuscripts faithfully represent the original text? This is the work of textual criticism. Scholars have concluded that the 5,000 extant manuscripts are about ninety-eight percent match on all major points. Some minor variations in terms of spelling, word order, or vocabulary can be found, but nothing that affects the meaning of a particular verse or passage ninety-eight percent of the time.[65] This is all the more remarkable given that these manuscripts were the work of many different copyists, working in different parts of the world over the course of several hundred years.

The extraordinarily low rate of variation between the thousands of New Testament manuscripts should not surprise us. Remember, the early Christians who passed on the Scriptures were copying the sacred texts they used for teaching, prayer, and worship. Indeed, they believed they were copying the very words of God himself. These manuscripts were copied with great care and reverence. In sum, the New Testament is the most reliable text we have from antiquity. We not only have tremendously more manuscripts of the New Testament than any other book from the ancient world; we also have a manuscript tradition that is purer than any other great work from that period. If the New Testament is not trustworthy, then no writings from the ancient world can be considered reliable. Not Homer, not Plato, not Cicero, not Caesar. If we cannot trust the New Testament manuscript tradition, then all university history and classics departments across the country would have no reliable documents from which to teach about the ancient world!

---

[65] The few more substantial variations do not affect doctrinal issues.

CHAPTER 9

Why Are Catholic Bibles Bigger?
The Old Testament and the Deuterocanonical Books

Catholic Bibles contain forty-six Old Testament books, while Protestant Bibles have only thirty-nine. What is the reason for this difference?

Simply put, Catholics distinguish between thirty-nine "protocanonical" books and seven "deuterocanonical" books of the Old Testament (i.e., Tobit, Judith, Wisdom, Sirach, Baruch, and 1-2 Maccabees). In many ways, this is an artificial distinction as both sets have been widely accepted and used by the Church from the beginning. The term *deuterocanonical* (meaning, "second canon") does not imply that these books are less canonical or a later addition to the Bible. Rather, the term was first used in the sixteenth century to distinguish those books from the other thirty-nine protocanonical books that were recognized in the Jewish and Christian traditions without much dispute. In contrast, the Scriptural character of the deuterocanonical works has at times been called into question.

Following the practice of many early Christians and the Church councils of the fourth century, the Council of Trent in 1546 defined the Old Testament canon as containing all forty-six books. Protestants, on the other hand, generally recognize only the thirty-nine protocanonical books as inspired and refer to the seven deuterocanonical books as *apocryphal* (meaning "hidden").

These books are often collectively referred to by Protestants as "the Apocrypha," and they are sometimes included at the end of Protestant versions of the Bible.

Protestant Bibles	Catholic Bibles
39 Old Testament Books	46 Old Testament Books
27 New Testament Books	27 New Testament Books

The Seven Deuterocanonical Books	
Tobit	Baruch
Judith	1 Maccabees
Wisdom of Solomon	2 Maccabees
Sirach	(Also portions of Daniel & Esther)

To appreciate the early Church's recognition of the seven deuterocanonical books, we must briefly examine the history of the Old Testament canon.

The Law, the Prophets, and the Writings

The Old Testament Scriptures were written over the course of at least a thousand years, and Judaism traditionally has divided its collection of sacred books into three parts:

1. The Law (*Torah*): The five books of the Bible (i.e., the Pentateuch): Genesis, Exodus, Leviticus, Numbers, and Deuteronomy.

2. The Prophets (*Nevi'im*): Includes what the Jews called "the former prophets" (the historical books running from

Joshua to Kings), and "the latter prophets" (the prophetic books from Isaiah to Malachi).

3. The Writings *(Kethubim)*: The most diverse assortment of books, including the Psalms; the wisdom literature, such as Proverbs, Ecclesiastes, Song of Songs, and Job; prophetic writings such as Lamentations and Daniel; and historical books, such as Ezra, Nehemiah, 1-2 Chronicles, and Esther.

This three-part structure was first alluded to in the prologue to Sirach, which was written around 132 BC when the original Hebrew text of Sirach was translated into Greek. However, the question about which books were considered authoritative remained open up to the time of Christ and beyond. The five books of the Law and the Prophets enjoyed widespread acceptance in first-century Judaism. But the third group remained more fluid. The book of Sirach referred to this section vaguely as "the Writings." Similarly, Jesus alluded to this third part of the Old Testament merely as "the Psalms" (Lk 24:44), and they were called "hymns and other works" by Philo and "hymns to God and precepts" by Josephus. The diversity and vagueness of titles for this section of Scripture point to a lack of precision in the first century about what kind of literature and which specific books were to be included here.[66]

A Loose Canon

In a process that began in the late first and second centuries AD, rabbinic Judaism eventually limited the canon to twenty-two books, which correspond to the thirty-nine protocanonical books in our Christian Bibles today.[67] However, in the time of Jesus, the

---

[66] R. Brown and R. Collins, "Canonicity," in *The New Jerome Biblical Commentary* (Englewood Cliffs, NJ: Prentice Hall, 1990), p. 1036.

[67] The twelve minor prophets were considered one book and other individual Old Testament books were similarly combined and counted as one. Many thus conclude that these twenty-two books correspond to the thirty-nine protocanonical books.

Jews did not yet have a sharply defined canon that excluded the deuterocanoncial books. In fact, Christianity was born in a period when the deuterocanonical books were still being used in many segments of Judaism.

For example, the first-century Jewish sect known as the Essenes had a much broader collection of sacred books than the twenty-two eventually found in later Jewish tradition. More than eight hundred scrolls and fragments were first discovered in 1947 at the site of their community at Qumran, near the Dead Sea. These scrolls (known as the Dead Sea Scrolls) show that they possessed a wide range of books, including almost all of the thirty-nine protocanonical books (all but Esther and Nehemiah) and even some deuterocanonical books (Tobit and Sirach and part of Baruch, known as the Letter of Jeremiah), along with other ancient non-biblical Jewish writings such as Jubilees and 1 Enoch. Given the varied collection of texts found at Qumran, there does not seem to be a closed canon of Scripture that was universally accepted in the first century. The Essenes at Qumran, at least, show no awareness of a closed canon, and they certainly did not exclude the deuterocanonical books.

Another indication of diversity in first-century Judaism in regard to which books were accepted as Scripture is the way some Jews (especially those in the Diaspora) used the Septuagint, the Greek translation of the Hebrew Scriptures. Compiled in the third and second centuries before Christ, the Septuagint included not only the thirty-nine protocanonical books but also the deuterocanonical books. Their full integration with the rest of Scripture also is seen in the early Church as reflected in the ancient bound copies (known as *codices*) of the Septuagint. Used for public worship, these bound copies did not separate the deuterocanonical books from the other works as if they were additions to the Jewish Scriptures. Rather, they were mixed with the Prophets and the Writings, which would seem to indicate that the Church viewed these books as having full standing in the Old Testament Scriptures.

The first clear indication of Jewish leaders limiting their

Scriptures to what we now call the protocanonical books is not found until near the end of the first century AD, when some writers begin attesting to twenty-four or twenty-two books of the Hebrew Bible. For example, the Jewish historian Josephus (writing about AD 90) mentions twenty-two books in the Jewish Scriptures, while an apocryphal work known as 4 Ezra (from about AD 100) refers to twenty-four sacred books. It is not clear, however, that Josephus reflects a universally held belief in Judaism regarding the canon, and his view on the matter comes near the end of the first century—long after the life of Christ and the emergence of the Christian Church.

Evidence that the Old Testament canon was still open in the first century AD can be found in how Jewish teachers continued to debate which books were a part of Scripture. Rabbis in Jamnia near the end of the first century debated whether Song of Songs and Ecclesiastes were inspired by God.[68] They do not seem to be aware of Josephus' demarcation of only twenty-two accepted books. Though this gathering at Jamnia was not an official council with authority over all Jews, the fact that leading rabbis were debating the issue suggests that the matter had not yet been completely settled.

Discussion among the rabbis about these and other books continued into the second century AD and beyond, as Jewish leaders argued even into the fifth century over whether Song of Songs, Ecclesiastes, Ezekiel, Proverbs, and Esther should be read in public.[69] Since the reading of biblical texts communicates their authority and sacredness, the fact that Jewish leaders were thinking of excluding these books from public reading indicates that the canon of Scripture for the Jews, though largely stabilized in the second century, was still not yet definitively fixed.

---

[68] *M. Yad.* 3:2-5.
[69] L.M. McDonald, *The Biblical Canon* (Peabody. MA: Hendrickson, 2007), pp. 176-7.

Christianity Did Not Inherit a Closed Canon

Given the lack of precision in the time of Christ about which Jewish books were authoritative, it should come as no surprise that the early Christian Church did not inherit an official Old Testament canon from Judaism. There was none. That being the case, most of the early Christian writers used a wide variety of Jewish texts, including the deuterocanonical books. The New Testament writers, for example, allude to Sirach, Wisdom, 1 & 2 Maccabees, and Tobit. Moreover, when the New Testament writers quote the Old Testament, more than ninety percent of the references are taken directly from the Septuagint, indicating at least a comfort with using a collection of Old Testament writings that included deuterocanoncial books. But the main point is this: The Jews in Jesus' day did not have a sharply defined canon and the deuterocanoncial books were not excluded by the Judaism from which Christianity was born. The early Christians received, accepted and used this wider collection of books—long before later Jewish rabbis began discussing which books were inspired and even before the limiting of the Old Testament books found in Josephus and 4 Ezra.

So there are two key questions: 1) Who determined which books were part of the Old Testament? and 2) By what authority did they do this? As we have seen, it was rabbis in the second century AD and beyond who played a crucial role in this process for the Jews, limiting their Scriptures to twenty-two books and determining which specific writings made up this twenty-two-book canon. From a Christian perspective, however, Jewish rabbis in the late first, second, and third centuries do not have authority for making such decisions for the Church in the Christian era. The earliest Christians received a wider range of texts that were being used by many Jews, as there was not yet a universally accepted narrowing of the Old Testament Scriptures among Jews at this time. This process did not begin for the Jews until near the end of the first century—long after the birth of Christianity and the Church. Therefore, from a Christian perspective, it was not Jewish rabbis in the late first and second century, but Christ's apostles and their successors who in the New Covenant era had authority to make such decisions. And the Church did just that. In her official teachings, the early Church affirmed the deuterocanonical books as part of the Old Testament canon, as we see in the Council of Rome (382) and the Councils of Hippo (393) and Carthage (397). Though doubts about the deuterocanonical books arose from time to time over the centuries (because they were not included in the later Jewish version of the Old Testament canon),[70] the Church never excluded them from the canon, and the majority of Christians continued to view them as authoritative for the first 1,500 years of Christianity.

The first time in Christianity that there was a widespread limiting of the Old Testament to only the thirty-nine protocanonical books came with the Protestant Reformation. When Martin Luther translated the Bible into German, he rejected the deuterocanonical books as Scripture, referring to them as "apocryphal" works that were "useful and good for reading" but not part of the canon of Scripture. Thus, his Old Testament contained only the thirty-nine protocanonical books. In response, the Council of Trent reaffirmed the early Church's teaching on the canonicity of the deuterocanonical books. Biblical scholar Raymond Brown has pointed out how Trent's acceptance of the wider canon ironically reflects the early Christian period more than Luther's exclusion of the deuterocanoncial books: "Curiously, Trent by accepting a wider canon seems to have preserved an authentic memory of the days of

---

[70] The earliest record we have of a Christian seeking to exclude the deuterocanonical books is Melito of Sardis in AD 170-190. He argued for the twenty-two Hebrew books, which match the twenty-two of the developing Jewish canon (which also correspond to the thirty-nine protocanonical books in modern Bibles). Though some other Church Fathers favored the twenty-two as well, the Church never excluded the deuterocanonical books.

Christian origins, whereas other Christian groups in a professed attempt to return to primitive Christianity have settled for a narrower Jewish canon that ... was the creation of a later period."[71]

---

[71] R. Brown and R. Collins, "Canonicity," in *The New Jerome Biblical Commentary* (Englewood Cliffs, NJ: Prentice Hall, 1990), p. 1042.

PART IV

BIBLICAL BACKGROUND

CHAPTER 10

Taking God at His Word: Is the Bible Trustworthy?

If the Bible is inspired by God, it has a unique authority. The Bible is not merely a record of one particular people's spiritual experiences or opinions about God. Nor is it merely yet another holy book among the many revered writings of the world's various religions. The fact that the Bible is inspired by God means that it is actually God's own word, the written witness of his revelation to humanity.

Since all of Scripture is inspired and has God as its author, the Church teaches that the Bible is without error. God, who is Truth itself, cannot author falsehood. Therefore, it is impossible for error to coexist with the divine inspiration of Scripture. Recall the perfect unity between the human writer's intention and God's will for the biblical text: the human writer "consigned to writing whatever he [God] wanted written, and no more."[72] Therefore, as Vatican II points out, the Bible must be without error: "Since therefore all that the inspired authors or sacred writers affirm should be regarded as affirmed by the Holy Spirit, we must acknowledge that the books of Scripture firmly, faithfully, and without error teach that truth which God, for the sake of our salvation, wished to see confided to the Sacred Scriptures."[73]

---

[72] CCC 106.
[73] CCC 107, citing DV 11.

Taking the Bible Literally?

Belief in the inerrancy of Scripture is "the ancient and unchanging faith of the Church."[74] Everything the biblical authors intend to affirm is true. But does this mean we should take the Bible *literally*? Here we must clarify what the Church means.

First, the Catholic view of Scripture is very different from the fundamentalist view, which reads the Bible in a *literalistic* way, considering only its surface meaning, apart from its literary genre or historical context. To discern the truth that God put in Scripture, we must remember that God speaks to us in a human way, through the human writers of the Bible. Therefore, as we saw in Chapter 3, we should carefully consider the author's intention—what the human author wanted to communicate in the text.[75] This is why the Church emphasizes that interpreters of the Bible should take into account the *historical context* in which the book was written, since certain words or actions reported in the Bible may have a particular meaning in the original ancient culture. We also should respect the *literary genre* the author employed. We should not read poetry as prose or a simile as a literal description. Rather, we should read metaphors metaphorically, laws legally, poems poetically, and history historically. Finally, we should consider the modes of *feeling, speaking,* and *narrating* used in biblical times, since the way ancient peoples reported history, told stories, or wrote letters is very different from the way we do today. In this way, the Catholic interprets Scripture the way one should approach any piece of literature: not "literalistically" but *literarily,* carefully examining the literary forms being used and seeking the author's intention. This helps us discern the truth that the author was intending to communicate in the biblical text.

---

[74]   *Providentissimus Deus* (PD) 20.
[75]   CCC 109.

Avoiding Fundamentalism

The fundamentalist, however, reads texts superficially in a literalistic way that does not respect the author's intention. This one-dimensional approach drains the rich meaning out of words by wrenching them out of their historical context. Such an approach fails to factor in the literary genre and artistry employed by the human authors of the Bible.

For example, when Christ warns, "If your right eye causes you to sin, pluck it out," he is using hyperbole. He is simply using a graphic illustration to show how crucial it is to root out the sin of lust from one's heart (Mt 5:29-30). A literalistic interpretation would wrongly conclude that Jesus is actually encouraging us to gouge our eye out if it leads us to sin! Similarly, when Psalm 73:20 describes God "awakening," this is not meant to teach that the Lord actually sleeps so that he needs to "wake up." This is figurative language used to describe how God, after remaining apparently unresponsive to a situation (from a purely human perspective, of course), suddenly begins to take action like a man awakening from sleep.

Science

In matters of natural science, the Church teaches that the sacred writers did not intend to teach astronomy, physics, or chemistry. They often used figurative language and terms commonly used at the time to describe what appeared to their senses.[76] Hence, in passages that depict the sun moving around the earth (Jos 10:12-13; Ps 19:5-6; Eccl. 1:5), or the moon as being larger than the stars of the sky (Gn 1:16), the sacred writers were not intending to give astronomy lessons. On the contrary, they were using common modes of expression that describe what appeared to the senses—and this they did accurately. As Pope Leo XIII explains, "[The sacred writers] did not seek to penetrate the secrets of nature, but rather described and dealt with things in more or less figurative

---

[76] PD 18.

language, or in terms which were commonly used at the time ...
Ordinary speech primarily and properly describes what comes
under the senses; and somewhat in the same way the sacred writers
... went by what sensibly appeared."[77]

People commonly speak this way, even today. When the
weatherman, for example, says the sun will set at six o'clock, we should
not accuse him of a colossal astronomical error. We understand that
he isn't offering a scientific description of the actual movement of the
sun but instead is using a common expression that describes a certain
time of day based on what appears to our senses. Likewise, we should
not view the Bible as making a scientific error when, for example,
it describes the sun "going down" (Gn 15:12). The sacred writer is
accurate in this statement, for he is not intending to teach science, but
rather, like the weatherman, is making use of a common expression to
denote a certain time of day and describe what the sun appears to be
doing at that time. So with passages such as these, it would not be the
Bible that is in error but the interpreter who mistakenly understands
this passage in a literalistic way.

History

As with matters of science, we must consider the writer's
intention in matters of history as well. If a writer is clearly
presenting an historical narrative, then the text should be
considered as faithfully presenting real, historical events; they are
not to be understood as being merely symbolic or figurative. This
does not mean the Bible's historical narratives should be read as
thoughtless, wooden reports of events. On the contrary, the biblical
writers put a lot more into their accounts than mere history. They
took into account their intended audience and the pastoral lessons
they wanted to communicate. They made decisions about which
traditions to report and which to leave out. They often made
theological observations and pointed out when events in their

---

[77] PD 18.

narratives fulfilled prophecy or related to other events in salvation history. They shaped their narratives with literary techniques common in their time and used their own creativity in the writing process. But all this ingenuity on the part of the human writer does not take away from the history found in their accounts.

Take, for example, the four gospels. The Church teaches that the gospels "faithfully hand on what Jesus, the Son of God, while he lived among men, really did and taught."[78] Even though the gospel writers selected which events from Jesus' life to report and explained those words and deeds of Christ with an eye to their communities, the gospels still present "the honest truth about Jesus."[79]

This means that the Gospel accounts of Jesus' miracles are to be taken as historical. Since the gospels are historical narratives intending to tell us about Christ's life, we can conclude that their accounts of Jesus' multiplication of loaves, healing of the blind men, and calming of the storm point to actual miraculous actions that Jesus performed. These accounts are not to be taken merely as legends created by the early Christians or as fictitious stories invented to make theological points about Jesus (i.e., he was divine; he fulfilled prophecy). Neither are the miracles to be explained away merely by some natural cause (e.g., Jesus didn't actually calm the storm: the weather improved at that moment by coincidence; Jesus didn't actually multiply the loaves and fishes: the people simply shared their bread and fish with one another, thus "multiplying" loaves through encouraging generosity). On the contrary, the gospel accounts of Jesus' miracles faithfully hand on what Jesus "really did and taught."[80]

Of course, the case is different if a biblical writer is using a parable or allegory to make a particular point. Take, for example, the parable of the good Samaritan (see Lk 10:29-37). From the literary form itself, it is clear that this story is not meant to be understood as an actual historical event. The story is simply a

---

[78] CCC 126, quoting DV 19.
[79] Ibid.
[80] Ibid.

parable Jesus used to expound on his teaching about loving one's neighbor. Nevertheless, Luke's gospel is an historical narrative, so we should conclude that Jesus' telling of the parable to his disciples was an historical event.

Dealing with Difficulties

There are dozens of difficult passages in the Bible which, at first glance, appear to contradict other Scriptural texts or seem to be in opposition to what we know from modern history and science. Most of these apparent contradictions can be easily explained; some are more difficult to resolve. The critical issue, however, is the attitude an interpreter of Scripture has when approaching an apparent discrepancy. Pope Pius XII, in his 1943 encyclical *Divino Afflante Spiritu*, taught that when we encounter difficulties in the Bible, we must keep in mind that *God put difficulties in the sacred texts in order to humble us*, so that we might trust more in him and his word than our own ability to understand the Scriptures. "God wished difficulties to be scattered through the Sacred Books inspired by him, in order that we might be urged to read and scrutinize them more intently, and, experiencing in a salutary manner our own limitations, we might be exercised in due submission of mind."[81]

In the end, the Church calls us to adopt a reverential attitude toward the Scriptures. When St. Augustine came across difficulties in the Bible—difficulties that even his great intellect could not resolve—he did not conclude that the inspired word of God was at fault. Rather than stand in judgment over the Scriptures, he humbly recognized his own limitations and concluded that perhaps he was working with a faulty manuscript or a poor translation or even that he might simply be lacking in understanding:

> On my own part I confess to your charity that it is only to those books of Scripture which are now called

---

[81] *Divino Afflante Spiritu* 45

canonical that I have learned to pay such honor and reverence as to believe most firmly that none of their writers has fallen into any error. And if in these books I meet anything which seems contrary to truth, I shall not hesitate to conclude either that the text is faulty [a defective copy of the Bible], or that the translator has not expressed the meaning of the passage, or that I myself do not understand.[82]

---

[82] St. Augustine, *Ep. lxxxii*, 1, as cited in PD 21.

CHAPTER 11

The World of the Bible: Archaeology, Geography, and History

To understand the message of the Bible, it is helpful to know something about the historical context in which the various sacred books were written. The biblical authors often mention peoples, places, customs, and events in passing, assuming that their original readers knew what they were referencing and understood their significance. Christian readers today, however, are far removed from the biblical world of Abraham, Moses, Jesus, and Paul. We might feel lost when the Bible lists a series of peoples and places we never learned about in history class or customs that are not a part of our daily lives. In order to understand better the *words* of the Bible, we must strive to learn more about the *world* of the Bible.

This chapter will provide a brief introduction to three tools students of the Bible often use to help them enter the biblical world: archaeology, geography, and history.

Archaeology: Digging Deeper in the Bible

Archaeology, the study of antiquity based on the recovery and examination of artifacts from the ancient world, combines a variety of disciplines such as history, geography, anthropology, linguistics, sociology, and even ceramics and medicine. It also uses a wide range of excavation methods such as radar, infrared photography, and computer analysis to recover, restore, and analyze artifacts from antiquity.

Biblical archaeology examines what can be learned about biblical events, characters, and customs from non-biblical sources in the ancient world. Archaeological studies can shed light on the Scriptures and help us understand the biblical world better. Archaeology cannot prove or disprove the theological claims made by the Scriptures (e.g., the existence of God, the divinity of Christ, etc.) since these supernatural truths go beyond the scope of archaeological science. But archaeology can confirm historical claims made by Scripture and provide more background to biblical accounts. For example, archaeological evidence can confirm what 2 Kings 17:3-6 reports: that the Assyrian ruler Shalmaneser besieged Samaria and captured it, which eventually led to the people being carried into exile. But archaeology cannot demonstrate what 2 Kings goes on to explain: this happened because the people sinned against the Lord (2 Kings 17:7-8). This is a theological claim, outside the scope of archaeology.

The contributions archaeology can make toward understanding the Bible are manifold. Since Scripture does not intend to offer a complete history of Israel, many historical records discovered in the ancient Near East can fill in some of the history that is not reported in the Scriptures. For example, 1 Kings 14:25-28 briefly mentions that the Egyptian King Shishak attacked Jerusalem and plundered the treasures in the Temple and the royal palace. This is reported to have taken place in the fifth year of Rehoboam's reign, shortly after the split of the powerful Davidic Kingdom into two smaller, weaker nations: the Northern Kingdom of Israel and the Southern Kingdom of Judah. This biblical account of Shishak's attack is confirmed by his own record of his conquest on a temple wall in Egypt, which lists about 150 cities taken in Judah and Samaria. A monument of Shishak also was discovered in Megiddo, further indicating his presence and conquest in the land of Judah. The archaeological data not only confirms the Scriptural account of Shishak's invasion, but also provides a broader context that shows the extent of damage inflicted in Judah and in the Northern Kingdom.

The recovery of objects from ancient Israel also can contribute to our understanding of the biblical world. Items such as coins, weights, measures, tools, jewelry, and weapons help us to know more about the customs of God's people and to know exactly what a word means. For example, Jesus speaks in the gospels about a "talent" or "shekel." Through the insights of archaeology, we now know precisely what those weights are.

Understanding the Patriarchs

Archaeology also sheds light on the laws and customs of the ancient Near East in a way that helps us understand biblical stories that might not make sense to some modern readers. For example, Genesis 15 tells how Abraham and Sarah were childless and intended to make their servant Eliezer their heir, like an adopted son. And Genesis 16 narrates Sarah giving Abraham her maidservant Hagar so that he could have a child by her. Archaeology sheds some light on these biblical accounts. Clay tablets discovered in the Mesopotamian city of Nuzi show that it was common for barren women to offer their maidservants as a concubine to their husbands and to adopt someone as an heir. The tablets also show laws protecting the parties involved. These tablets were written just a few centuries after the time Abraham and Sarah were reported to have lived and probably reflect ancient customs with which they would have been familiar from their own upbringing in Mesopotamia before moving to the land of Canaan.

In addition, archaeology gives us a broader understanding of the New Testament world. For example, the Bible presents Herod the Great as the violent and wicked king ruling at the time of Jesus' birth, but besides the account of the Magi visiting Herod and his ordering the massacre of the male children in Bethlehem (see Mt 2), few details about his life are given. A broader view of his life can be found in the writings of the first-century Jewish historian Josephus and through the work of archaeologists who have unearthed many of the massive palaces and buildings constructed during his reign. One of the most prolific builders in the Roman world of his time, Herod left behind fortresses, palaces, aqueducts, and even whole cities that pilgrims can visit today. Coins bearing his name, the city of Caesarea along the sea, the fortress of Masada, his palaces at Jericho and Herodium, and the thirty-five-acre platform for the Jerusalem Temple all are artifacts pointing to how dominant a ruler Herod was.

Athletes and Celery

The letters of St. Paul also can be better understood in light of archaeological research. For example, Paul's first letter to the Corinthians uses popular athletic images that would have resonated with his original readers. Through archaeology, we know that Corinth was famous for hosting the athletic festival known as the Isthmian Games, which ranked second only to the Olympic Games in the ancient world. These games brought large numbers of outsiders into Corinth every two years. The population grew so much that visitors stayed around the city in tents. Thus, when Acts 18:3 reports that Paul worked as a tent-maker in Corinth, he was probably making tents for visitors coming to the Isthmian Games.

This background also helps us better understand Paul's words in 1 Corinthians 9:24-25: "Do you not know that in a race all the runners compete, but only one receives the prize? So run that you may obtain it. Every athlete exercises self-control in all things." Here, Paul describes the Christian path as a race with athletes in training who discipline themselves in self-control in order to win a prize. When Paul's letters are read in light of the Isthmian Games that were at the center of Corinthian culture, we can more powerfully feel the force of his words to the sports-crazed Corinthians. It would be like a modern preacher using football metaphors on Super Bowl Sunday or race-car imagery in Indianapolis in May to describe the Christian way.

Finally, consider Paul's words in 1 Corinthians 9:25, where he contrasts the runners who pursue "a perishable wreath" with the Christians who seek "an imperishable" one. This image takes on greater force when we realize that the winners of the Corinthian games were awarded a crown made of withering celery! Paul is basically saying that if runners in training for the Isthmian games work so hard to discipline their bodies in order to win a crown of celery (!), how much more should Christians make sacrifices and discipline themselves, for they pursue an imperishable crown of reigning with Christ in heavenly glory.

Geography: The Stage for the Drama

The Bible tells the story of God's saving work with real people who lived in certain locations during specific moments in history. Therefore, the geographical and cultural setting of the many people in the Bible serves as the stage on which the divine drama unfolds.

Geography helps shape the life and culture of a people. A region's terrain, climate, raw materials, and water sources largely determine the kind of settlements, agriculture, trade, and lifestyles that may arise there. Location also can influence a people's political position, military alliances, and ability to trade with other societies. Thus, the more we learn about the geographical setting of the biblical world, the more we will understand the peoples of the Bible and God's dealings with them.

The Center of the World

Medieval Christian geographers sometimes presented Jerusalem as the center of the world. Though a modern cartographer would say this was bad geography, this medieval view did express an important theological truth: The God of the universe chose to enter the story of the human family with one particular group of people (the Jews), in one particular region of the world (Palestine), at one particular period of time (the first century). And the climax of this story occurred at one particular spot just outside the walls of Jerusalem—the place where Jesus was crucified and buried. That moment at that place was the turning point of the history of the world. Thus, Jerusalem is indeed the center of the drama of salvation.

The land where Jesus dwelt is commonly called "Palestine." In Scripture, this land of the Jews was often a converging point for peoples from three different continents: Africa, Asia, and Europe. On the one hand, this land was invaded by nations from all three of these continents (Africa: Egypt; Asia: Assyria and Babylon; Europe: Greece and Rome). On the other hand, it was from this land placed somewhat at the center of ancient civilization that Christ's kingdom went out to all three continents and the rest of the world.

The Fertile Crescent

Most of the story of Scripture took place in an area known as "the Fertile Crescent." This was a span of land in the ancient Near East that had good water sources and a favorable climate and terrain for agricultural development. Hence, many settlements sprung up in this area. The Fertile Crescent stretched from the Persian Gulf through Mesopotamia (present-day northeast Iraq and northern Syria) to the southern part of present-day Turkey. It then turns south through a small strip of land along the Mediterranean Sea, down to the southern part of Palestine (see Map 1).

Within the northern and eastern part of the Fertile Crescent, Mesopotamia played an important role in the Old Testament story. It was the home of Abraham and the setting for parts of other stories in Genesis about the patriarchs. Later in the Old Testament, this region became the home of the Assyrian and Babylonian empires,

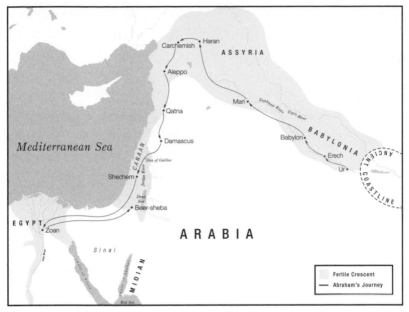

Map 1: The Fertile Crescent and Abraham's Journey

which invaded the land of Palestine and took many Israelites back to Mesopotamia in exile.

South and west of the Fertile Crescent in the northwest corner of Africa lies Egypt, best known for being the setting for the Exodus story. Egypt also was the stage for other biblical events, including a scene in the life of Abraham, the rise of the patriarch Joseph, and the relocation of Jacob's family during a great famine in Genesis. Later in the Old Testament, Egyptian kingdoms interact with God's people, sometimes as allies against mutual foes and sometimes as enemies invading the land of Palestine. From at least the time of the Babylonian exile (sixth century BC), Egypt became a popular place for Jewish refugees. A large Jewish population dwelt there at the end of the Old Testament period.

The land of Israel is the center of God's dealings with his chosen people in the Old Testament. This is the land of the patriarchs in Genesis—the land originally promised to Abraham, in which he resided after leaving Mesopotamia. It is the place the Israelites re-entered and possessed after being liberated from slavery in Egypt (see

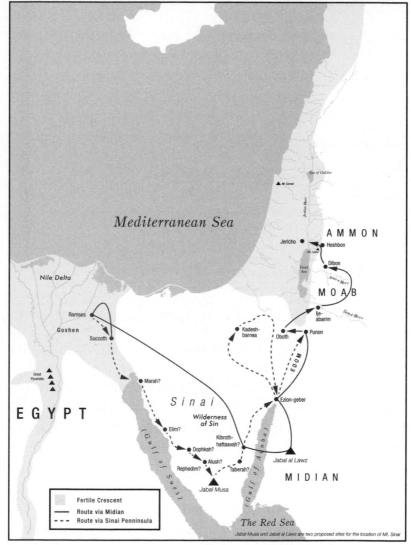

Map 2: Exodus, Wilderness Wanderings, and the Promised Land

Map 2). It is also the place from which the Davidic Kingdom grew and
expanded. When the kingdom was split into two, the Promised Land
itself was divided into two regions: Samaria in the north (possessed
by the ten tribes of the northern Kingdom of Israel) and Judah in the
south (possessed by the southern Kingdom of Judah) (see Map 3).

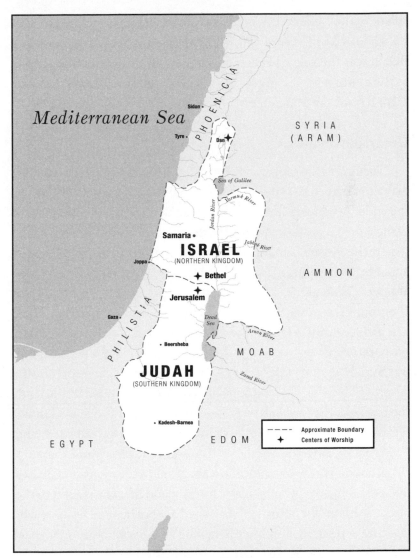

Map 3: Kingdoms of Israel and Judah

The wider Mediterranean world took on greater importance in the latter part of the Old Testament, especially with the expansion of the Greek empire, which brought the Greek language and culture into the land of the Jews. After the death of Alexander the Great, the Greek empire was divided into four parts. The Jews were first ruled by the Ptolemaic Kingdom (based in Egypt) from 320-198 BC, followed by the Seleucid dynasty (based in Syria) from 198-143 BC. It was the Seleucid persecution of Jews in 167 BC that served as the context for the Maccabean Revolt reported in the first and second books of Maccabees.

Geography and Jesus

Turning to the geography of the New Testament, we see that two main areas emerge: 1) the land of the Jews where Jesus dwelt, and 2) the wider Mediterranean world where the Church expands in Acts of the Apostles, primarily through the missionary journeys of Paul.

In the Gospel accounts of Christ's public ministry, we read about Jesus traveling in Galilee, Judea, Samaria, and the Decapolis, among other regions. These different regions were home to different groups (i.e., Jews, Samaritans, Gentiles). In addition, they often had different rulers (e.g., Herod Antipas ruled Galilee, the Roman procurator Pilate governed Judea and Samaria, and the Decapolis was Syrian territory). Jesus passed through a wide range of terrain: desert wilderness, mountainous hill country, cultivated fertile land, the banks of the Jordan River, and the shores of the Sea of Galilee. He also took his public ministry into cities such as Jerusalem and Capernaum, as well as smaller villages like Nazareth and Cana.

Knowing the geographical background to the events in Christ's life—the kinds of people, rulers, terrain, and lifestyles found in the places of his public ministry—can shed a lot of light on Jesus' teachings and actions. For example, when he asks his followers in Capernaum to cross the Sea of Galilee with him and go to the Decapolis, understanding the geography of the Holy Land helps us to see this is no simple, leisurely day-trip. Jesus is calling his disciples to leave their homes and travel with him into Gentile territory. This move is intended to separate the true disciples who are willing to join Jesus on this difficult "foreign mission" from the enthusiastic crowds who are merely impressed with Christ's healing miracles (see Mt 8:18-22).

Another case in point is Jesus' travels northeast of the Sea of Galilee that brought him into the region of Gaulanitis and the jurisdiction of Herod Antipas' brother, Philip. This area had a largely Gentile population and was not as politically volatile as Galilee. With this geographical background in mind, we might conclude that Jesus

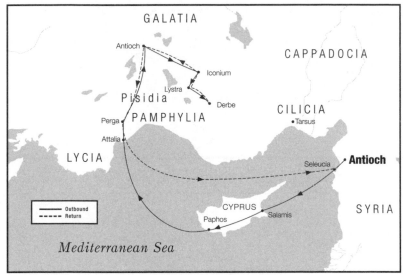

Map 4: Paul's First Journey

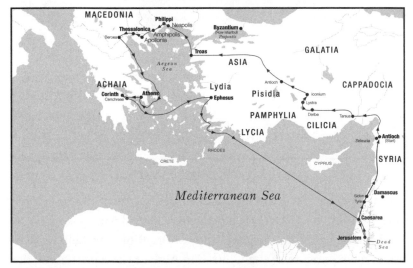

Map 5: Paul's Second Journey

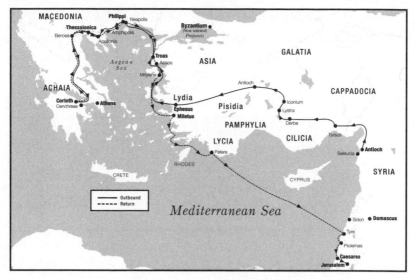

Map 6: Paul's Third Journey

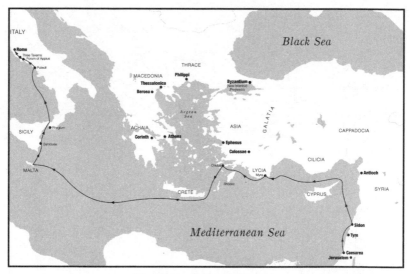

Map 7: Paul's Fourth Journey

withdrew there in order to seek occasional rest from the large crowds of Jews in Galilee and to avoid the hand of Herod Antipas.

Finally, knowing the geography of the Bible can help readers trace the expansion of the Church in Acts of the Apostles, as the kingdom spreads from Jerusalem (Acts 1-7) to Judea and Samaria

(Acts 8) and to the ends of the earth (Acts 9-28; see Acts 1:8). This is particularly true for understanding Paul's life, letters, and missionary journeys. Here, the biblical drama moves out of Palestine and into Asia Minor (present-day Turkey) and Greece and, ultimately, all the way to Rome, the capital of the Empire (see Maps 4-7).

Ancient Rabbis & Lost Scrolls: The Value of Non-Biblical Sources

Non-biblical Jewish texts dating from the centuries before and after Christ can be helpful for shedding light on the Jewish world of Jesus' day. They also provide valuable information for filling in the historical timeline from the period of the Maccabees to the early Church. These non-biblical Jewish writings also are helpful resources for understanding ancient Jewish methods of interpreting the Old Testament, the meaning of certain words and concepts that appear in the New Testament, and the historical, social, and religious context for Christ's ministry and the growth of the Church.

This section will provide a brief introduction to some of the most famous non-biblical writings used by scholars to assist them in their interpretation of Scripture: 1) the Dead Sea Scrolls; 2) the writings of the Jewish historian Josephus; 3) the writings of the Jewish commentator Philo; and 4) the many rabbinic writings such as the Mishnah, Tosefta, Talmuds, and Targums.

The Dead Sea Scrolls

The Dead Sea Scrolls refer to the some eight hundred scrolls and fragments of ancient manuscripts discovered between 1947 and 1957 in caves from the Qumran area along the western shore of the Dead Sea in Israel. These manuscripts were written or copied between 200 BC and AD 70, and the majority of scholars conclude they were the product of the Jewish sect called the Essenes.

The contents of the Dead Sea Scrolls can be divided into three categories: 1) copies of almost every Old Testament book; 2) non-biblical writings such as 1 Enoch, Jubilees, and the Testaments of the

Patriarchs; and 3) the community's own documents, which included commentaries on Jewish Scriptures, rules for community conduct, and prayers and hymns used for the community's worship. These documents provide valuable information about the Old Testament and the first-century Jewish world from which Christianity emerged.

First, almost all of the protocanonical books (all except Esther and Nehemiah) are represented in the Dead Sea Scrolls. Prior to the discovery of the Dead Sea Scrolls, the earliest Old Testament manuscripts dated from around the year 1000. Now, scholars have at least fragmentary textual evidence of many Old Testament books—and even some whole Old Testament books—dating from around the first century. Moreover, while the deuterocanonical books Tobit and Sirach were handed down in the Greek Septuagint, the Dead Sea Scrolls provide portions of Sirach in Hebrew and Tobit in Aramaic.

Second, the Aramaic commentaries on some Old Testament books (known as *Targums*) from the Dead Sea Scrolls help us have a better view of how the ancient Jews understood their Scriptures.

Third, the many documents pertaining to the Essene community and even the apocryphal texts kept at Qumran (such as 1 Enoch or Jubilees) shed light on the diversity of theological outlook among some Jews around the time of Christ.

Fourth, scholars have pointed out many parallels between the key themes in the Essene writings and features in early Christianity. Both emphasize the coming of the Messiah, the need for Israel to repent, the corruption of the Temple in Jerusalem, ritual washing as an initiation into the community, a sacred meal with bread and wine, celibacy as an ideal, and the place of the desert for God's eschatological plan to begin (see Is 40:3; Mt 3:1-3). Most of all, the Dead Sea Scrolls give us insight into one sect within Judaism claiming to be the true Israel and the faithful community where God would enact his eschatological plan. Studying the beliefs and practices of the Essenes, therefore, can shed light on how Christianity—another sect within Judaism claiming to be the true

Israel—might have grown out of the first-century Jewish world into its own independent movement.

Josephus

The works of Flavius Josephus are the most important collection of non-biblical writings for providing background to the New Testament and early Christianity. Josephus was a Jew born in AD 37 or 38 who studied Jewish law and became the leader of a Galilean army during the first revolt against Rome. He surrendered to Roman forces in the year 67. When released in AD 69, Josephus became an advisor to the Roman general Titus in the war upon Jerusalem. After the war, Josephus lived in Rome and acquired Roman citizenship. There, he began writing his works, including the *Jewish War*, which relates the events leading up to the Jewish revolt and the war itself, and the *Jewish Antiquities*, which chronicles the history of the Jewish people from Adam all the way up to the war against Rome. He also wrote *Against Apion* and his *Life* (a short autobiography appended to the *Antiquities*).

These works are important for biblical studies because they represent the most extensive non-biblical sources for understanding first-century Jewish history, politics, and sects. They provide a window into the Jewish world of Jesus and the apostles. Josephus' writings also tell us more about various groups, institutions, customs, places, and events that are only mentioned in passing in the New Testament. For example, Josephus gives an account of the origins, beliefs, and activities of the Pharisees and Sadducees. This background can round out the New Testament picture of these groups and help us better understand their opposition to Jesus, and in return, Jesus' critique of them. Also, Josephus depicts the Jewish high priests in the first century as corrupt and as collaborators with Rome, which fits with the New Testament presentation of Caiaphas. He also describes the hostility between Jews and Samaritans—something that the New Testament simply assumes. His detailed account of the Jewish war against Rome and the destruction of Jerusalem fit Jesus' warnings of judgment on the city and the Temple. Josephus' writings are also important because they hand on traditional Jewish interpretations of Old Testament texts.

Philo

Philo Judaeus (commonly known as Philo of Alexandria) was a Jewish writer who lived in Alexandria, Egypt, around the time of Christ (20 BC–AD 50). He is most famous for his allegorical interpretation of the Old Testament. Philo interpreted institutions, passages, and characters from the Old Testament in an allegorical way. For example, he viewed the Genesis account of Abraham leaving his home to go to the land of Canaan as Abraham turning away from the base desires of his body and turning his mind toward God. Similarly, the Adam in Genesis 1 is created in the image and likeness of God; he is "heavenly man" who remains perfect. The Adam of Genesis 2, however, was formed from the earth and had sensual desire, which clouded his reason and led him to fall. Philo explained that anyone who desires to be a son of God must imitate the man created in God's image. Philo's allegorical approach to the Bible can shed light on some New Testament passages that similarly interpret the Old Testament allegorically.

Jewish Pseudepigraphical Writings

There were many non-canonical Jewish writings composed in the period immediately before and shortly after the coming of Christ that were presented under names of great heroes of the Old Testament. These works are described as pseudepigraphical (meaning "falsely superscribed") because they were written under a false name. Some of these writings are: *1 Enoch, Jubilees, the Testaments of the Twelve Patriarchs, 4 Ezra, Psalms of Solomon,* and *2 Baruch.* Though not part of the canon of inspired Scripture, these writings bear witness to some diversity of thought in the Judaism of

Jesus' day. They also include themes, images, and ideas that relate to aspects of the New Testament. The letter of Jude 14-15 explicitly refers to 1 Enoch 1:9, and other New Testament texts may show awareness of other pseudepigraphical writings.[83]

Rabbinic Literature

Though Judaism was by and large an oral culture in Jesus' day, rabbis in the early third century began compiling the rabbinic oral traditions about case law, customs, and interpretations of the Mosaic law into one written source called the *Mishnah*. Edited by Rabbi Judah ha-Nasi around AD 200-220, the Mishnah codifies these oral traditions of the sages and rabbis from about 50 BC to AD 200. Later in the third century, additional rabbinic opinion was compiled and arranged following the order of the Mishnah in what is called the *Tosefta* (which means "addition" or "supplement"). The Tosefta includes some earlier traditions left out of the Mishnah and new interpretations and cases that developed in the generation or two after the Mishnah was compiled. It also expands and comments on items specifically addressed in the Mishnah.

Later rabbis developed commentaries on the Mishnah. The *Palestinian Talmud* (AD 400) and the *Babylonian Talmud* (AD 500) represent rabbinic opinion on the Mishnah from AD 200-500. Finally, a *targum* is an Aramaic paraphrase translation of the Hebrew Scriptures. These interpretive translations have their origins in the synagogues, but it is not certain how early these documents are. Evidence of targums at Qumran and Cairo Genizah has led scholars to conclude that the targums preserve some Jewish traditions that go back to the time of the New Testament.

In conclusion, some of the traditions in the rabbinic writings can be traced back to first-century Judaism and thus can shed light on certain New Testament passages. At the same time, scholars today are cautious about the use of rabbinic literature to make

---

[83] See McDonnald, *The Biblical Canon*, p. 195.

conclusions about the first-century Jewish world since these writings represent only one strand in the Jewish tradition (Pharisaic Judaism). In addition, they were compiled long after the time of Christ, later in the second and third centuries.

CHAPTER 12

Knowing God's Story:
The Twelve Periods of Biblical History

Many Christians have a "Humpty Dumpty" understanding of the Bible. We might be familiar with various stories from Scripture, such as the flood, the battle of David and Goliath, and the conversion of Paul. We might recognize key figures such as Abraham, Solomon, Esther, and Mary. But do we see clearly how all of these individual characters and stories fit together? Like Humpty Dumpty, our understanding of the Bible might consist of several scattered, individual pieces that cannot be put together again into a coherent whole.

The Bible does contain many individual prophecies, laws, letters, and narratives, but each of these smaller pieces is actually part of the overall story of salvation. In this chapter we will consider what a narrative approach to studying the Bible is and how it can help us see the whole, not just the individual parts. This is especially important for beginners. Readers who quickly grasp the "big picture" of salvation history—the overarching narrative from Adam to Christ and the Church—will possess a framework for better understanding all the other books of the Bible. With this narrative framework in mind, readers will get much more mileage out of their study of the sacred page. Without such a framework, Scripture study is more susceptible to becoming confused, fragmented, and broken—much like Humpty Dumpty.

From Genesis to Revelation?

A person who picks up the Bible for the first time hoping to read from Genesis to Revelation might quickly find himself somewhat lost and frustrated. He probably starts off well in the opening book of Genesis, which has many interesting stories that are relatively easy to follow: the temptation of Adam and Eve, Noah and the Flood, the call of Abraham, and the saga of Joseph's being sold into slavery and his rise to power in Egypt.

The beginner's passion for reading Scripture probably intensifies as he begins the second book of the Bible, Exodus, which opens with several dramatic, attention-grabbing events: babies thrown into the river Nile, God appearing in a burning bush, ten plagues falling on Egypt, and the parting of the Red Sea.

The first-time reader, however, encounters some initial bumps in the road in the latter part of Exodus, which presents seventeen chapters consisting almost entirely of long lists of laws and instructions, many of which are reported twice. He finally gets out of these legal chapters of Exodus and starts afresh with a new book, which he hopes will be much more engaging. And what does he find? The book of Leviticus! Here, he encounters chapter after chapter of detailed laws about how to sacrifice an animal for a burnt offering, the purification of women who became ritually unclean, and the consecration of Levitical priests. At this point, many first-time readers give up. Why bother wading through hundreds of obscure ceremonies, customs, and laws that seem to have very little to do with our lives today?

Indeed, the Bible does not read like a modern novel that unfolds a story chapter-by-chapter. Nor is it structured like a history book, chronologically walking readers through various historical periods.

Rather, the Bible consists of seventy-three books that are grouped in large part by literary style—historical books, poetry, wisdom literature, prophecy, and letters—not by a strict chronology. The connection between a psalm, an historical book, a certain prophecy, and a letter of St. Paul is not readily apparent.

The "Big Picture" of the Bible

To lay a solid foundation for personal Scripture study, it is important to focus on the "big picture" of the Bible—the central narrative thread that unites all seventy-three books and shows how they fit into the one divine drama of salvation. In this regard, while all books of the Bible are important, some books stand out for their ability to carry the narrative forward for readers chronologically, from one period in Israel's history to the next. These narrative books can serve as the backbone for understanding and contextualizing all the other books of the Bible.

Of the narrative books of the Old Testament, twelve are particularly helpful for telling the story straight through: Genesis, Exodus, Numbers, Joshua, Judges, 1 Samuel, 2 Samuel, 1 Kings, 2 Kings, Ezra, Nehemiah, 1 Maccabees. To this, two New Testament books could be added to carry the biblical narrative to its climax in the New Covenant era: Luke and Acts.[84] Reading these narrative books can provide an initial, general chronological knowledge of the history of Israel and the beginning of the Christian Church. This framework then can help contextualize all of the other books of the Bible: the psalms, the prophets, the wisdom books, laws, and letters.

Know the Story: The Twelve Periods of Biblical History

In conclusion, we will consider how the overall story of Scripture contained in the narrative books can be divided into twelve

---

[84] Since Luke's gospel was written by the same author as Acts, Luke and Acts are a good match for presenting the life of Christ (Luke) and the early Church (Acts) through a common lens.

major historical periods, moving from the Early World and the Patriarchs in Genesis, through the periods of the Royal Kingdom and Divided Kingdom in 1 & 2 Samuel and 1 & 2 Kings, and into the periods of Messianic Fulfillment and the Church in Luke and Acts. These periods trace the Bible's overarching storyline from one key narrative book to the next, from the Old Testament to the New. At the same time, knowing these twelve periods can help us contextualize all the other books of the Bible. By linking each of the other Scriptural books (the Psalms, prophets, laws, letters, etc.) to the twelve historical periods, we can see more clearly the particular role they play in the overall story of salvation.

Since understanding this biblical history is crucial for reading Scripture, we will offer a brief introduction to each of these twelve periods, noting the particular narrative books that cover each period as well as the other books of the Bible that are associated with each epoch.

Timeline Period	Narrative Book(s)	Supplemental Book(s)
Early World	*Genesis 1-11*	none
Patriarchs	*Genesis 12-50*	*Job*
Egypt & Exodus	*Exodus*	*Leviticus*
Desert Wanderings	*Numbers*	*Deuteronomy*
Conquest & Judges	*Joshua, Judges*	*Ruth*
Royal Kingdom	*1-2 Samuel, 1 Kings 1-11*	*Psalms, 1-2 Chronicles, Proverbs, Ecclesiastes, Song of Solomon*
Divided Kingdom	*1 Kings 12-22, 2 Kings*	*2 Chronicles, Obadiah, Joel, Amos, Jonah, Hosea, Isaiah, Micah*
Exile	*2 Kings*	*Tobit, Nahum, Habakkuk, Daniel, Ezekiel, Judith, Lamentations, Jeremiah, Zephaniah, Baruch*
Return	*Ezra, Nehemiah*	*Zechariah, Haggai, Esther, Malachi*
Maccabean Revolt	*1 Maccabees*	*2 Maccabees, Wisdom, Sirach*
Messianic Fulfillment	*Luke*	*Matthew, Mark, John*
The Church	*Acts*	*Paul's Letters, Other New Testament Letters, Revelation*

Early World

Narrative Book: Genesis 1-11

This first period introduces the plot for the drama of Scripture. God created man and woman in his image and likeness to be his children and share in his life. But tempted by the devil, they lacked trust in God's goodness and committed the first sin (CCC 397), destroying the original union they had had with God and with each other. The subsequent narratives of Genesis 4-11 underscore the further breakdown of the human family, culminating in the tower of Babel episode—a scene that offers a bleak picture of Adam and Eve's descendants rebelling against God and divided against each other.

Patriarchs

Narrative Book: Genesis 12-50
Supplemental Book: Job

God responds to the problem of the divided human family by raising up one particular family to heal, bless, and reunite the rest of the world back into covenant with him: the descendants of Abraham. In Genesis 12:1-3, God makes three promises that serve as a table of contents for the rest of the Bible. He promises that Abraham's descendants will become a great nation, have a great name (a dynasty), and become the source of blessing for all nations. These promises point to future fulfillment when Abraham's descendants (the Israelites) become a great nation in the time of Moses, a great kingdom in the time of David, and the instrument for blessing the rest of the world through Jesus Christ and his Church. Genesis 12-50 recounts how God's promise to rescue humanity passes from Abraham to Isaac to Jacob. The latter chapters tell how Jacob's family end up in Egypt during a famine—setting up the context for the next book of the Bible, Exodus.

Egypt & Exodus

Narrative Book: Exodus
Supplemental Book: Leviticus

This biblical period features Abraham's descendants becoming a holy nation as God rescues them from slavery in Egypt and brings them into the desert to make his covenant with them at Mount Sinai. There they receive the Ten Commandments and their mission to be a kingdom of priests, leading the other nations to God (Ex 19:6). Israel's covenant union with the Lord, however, is short-lived, as the people fall into idolatry, worshipping the golden calf. This apostasy marks a radical rupture in Israel's relationship with the Lord—and leads to the introduction of a new Levitical priesthood and a series of ceremonial, sacrificial laws intended to address the problem of Israel's sin.

Desert Wanderings

Narrative Book: Numbers
Supplemental Book: Deuteronomy

In this fourth period, the book of Numbers chronicles God's dealings with Israel during their journey in the wilderness from Sinai to the edge of the Promised Land. This period is marked by Israel's repeated failures—their unwillingness to trust God to provide for them, their rebellion against Moses' leadership, and their falling into pagan idolatry. Throughout these forty years, nearly all the Israelites from the first generation that escaped from Egypt die and a new generation arises, hoping to enter the land promised to their great ancestor Abraham. When this second generation falls into idolatry, failing to learn from the sins of their parents, God has Moses issue the covenant of Deuteronomy, which sets the parameters for Israel's relationship with the Lord in the Promised Land. If Israel is faithful to the covenant, they will be blessed in the land. But if they are unfaithful to the covenant, they will experience the curse of exile (Dt 28). Just as Adam and Eve were expelled from the Garden because of their sin, so Israel will be driven from the land if they break covenant with God.

Conquest & Judges

Narrative Books: Joshua, Judges
Supplemental Book: Ruth

The book of Joshua recounts Israel's entry into the Promised Land, their various battles with the Canaanites, and their eventual settling in the land near the end of Joshua's life. Possessing a land of their own, the people of Israel have become a nation, as God foretold in his first promise to Abraham (Gn 12:1-2; Jos 21:43-45). But dark shadows loom on the horizon. Whereas signs of Israel's weak spiritual condition can be seen in the book of Joshua, the people's blatant unfaithfulness comes to the forefront in the book of Judges. Without a strong spiritual leader like Joshua or Moses, the people in this period fall deeper into the sins of the pagans around them. Seven times Israel falls into sin, is oppressed by a foreign nation, and then cries out to God for help. Each time God raises up a "judge" to help them drive off their enemies, but the people fail to repent. As the book progresses, Israel is seen falling into a downward death-spiral that culminates in a violent, decadent, and relativistic society in which "every man did what was right in his own eyes" (Jgs 21:25).

Royal Kingdom

Narrative Books: 1-2 Samuel, 1 Kings 1-11
Supplemental Books: Psalms, 1-2 Chronicles, Proverbs, Ecclesiastes, Song of Solomon

The kingdom of Israel does not get off to a good start. The people initially ask God for a king "like all the nations" (1 Sam 8:4)— more of a political and militaristic leader than a spiritual one. As a result, the people get King Saul, a proud, insecure ruler who is more concerned with his own interests than with leading the people to

God. After Saul's failures in leadership, God raises up another man to be king: David, a man after God's own heart.

God makes a covenant with David, promises him an everlasting kingdom, and gives him a great name, signaling that the second promise to Abraham about a great name/dynasty is coming to fulfillment (see Gn 12:2; 2 Sam 7:9). After David makes Jerusalem his capital city, he begins expanding his kingdom's rule over other nations. This expansion continues with David's son, Solomon, who builds the Temple and brings Israel to its highest point so far. Foreign nations seek to make alliances with Solomon and learn from the wisdom God gave him. In Solomon's kingdom, therefore, we catch a glimpse of what Israel was always meant to be: a kingdom of priests, leading other nations to the wisdom of the one true God. However, Solomon marries pagan women, falls into idolatry, and begins taxing and enslaving the people. Though Solomon originally brings Israel to its highest point in its history, he is now leading the people quickly toward their lowest point.

Divided Kingdom

Narrative Books: 1 Kings 12-22, 2 Kings
Supplemental Books: 2 Chronicles, Obadiah, Joel, Amos, Jonah, Hosea, Isaiah, Micah

In the generation after Solomon, the kingdom splits in two, with the ten northern tribes of Israel rebelling against the Davidic dynasty and separating from God's Temple in Jerusalem. The northern tribes become known as the Kingdom of Israel, while the two southern tribes remaining in union with the Davidic dynasty become known as the Kingdom of Judah. 1 Kings 12-22 and 2 Kings chronicle the sin and corruption of these two kingdoms and their eventual demise, as foreign nations prepare to invade the land and carry the people off into exile. This period also witnesses the rise of many prophets calling the people to repent and warning them of God's judgment. Some of these prophetic ministries are mentioned in 1 and 2 Kings and some prophets have their own books, which are set in this time period and the next.

Exile

Narrative Book: 2 Kings
Supplemental Books: Tobit, Nahum, Habakkuk, Daniel, Ezekiel, Judith, Lamentations, Jeremiah, Zephaniah, Baruch

This period marks one of the lowest points in Israel's history, as the northern tribes in the Kingdom of Israel are sent into exile and scattered among the nations by Assyria (722 BC) and the southern tribes in the Kingdom of Judah are taken over by Babylon, which destroys the Temple and carries the people away as slaves. From a human perspective, the future of God's people looks bleak. Because they broke covenant with Yahweh, they lost the land and the kingdom that was promised them and are now scattered in exile among the nations—just as Moses foretold in the curses of Deuteronomy. But the prophets in this period offer a message of hope: One day soon God will bring them back to the land and eventually send a new son of David to restore Israel and the kingdom and fulfill his promise to bless all nations through Abraham's family.

Return

Narrative Books: Ezra, Nehemiah
Supplemental Books: Zechariah, Haggai, Esther, Malachi

In three major waves between 538 and 444 BC, Jews begin returning from Babylon to Jerusalem to rebuild their city and their temple. Without a Davidic king to rule them, the people are led by priests like Ezra and laymen like Nehemiah in the rebuilding of Jerusalem. The prophets in this period encourage the Jews to persevere in their rebuilding projects despite obstacles and foreign opposition, and they also point to the future when the Lord will come to rescue his people from their oppressors and restore the Davidic kingdom.

Maccabean Revolt

Narrative Book: 1 Maccabees
Suppplemental Books: 2 Maccabees, Wisdom, Sirach

Under Syrian rule in this period, the Jews face the most severe, systematic persecution thus far in their history. The Seleucid ruler Antiochus Epiphanes IV outlaws most of the distinctive features of Jewish belief, piety, and life in an effort to force the people to assimilate into the Greek culture around them. 1 Maccabees chronicles the resistance movement led by one family that is successful in driving the Seleucids out of Jerusalem and cleansing the Temple of idolatry.

Messianic Fulfillment

Narrative Book: Luke
Supplemental Books: Matthew, Mark, John

The gospel of Luke narrates the coming of the Messiah—the long-awaited royal son of David who will fulfill all prophecy, restore the kingdom to Israel, and gather all the nations back into covenant with God. Luke shows how Jesus' announcement of the kingdom in Galilee lays the foundation for the Church Christ is establishing; his death and resurrection in Jerusalem brings God's plan of salvation to its climax as Jesus takes upon himself the suffering of humanity and rises victoriously over death in order to free us from sin and enable us to share in eternal life in his kingdom. Through Christ and his Church, the third promise to Abraham is finally fulfilled as the blessing for the human family begins going out to all the earth.

The Church

Narrative Book: Acts
Supplemental Books: Paul's Letters, Other New Testament Letters, Revelation

This final period of biblical history shows how the apostles serve as witnesses to Christ's Kingdom, expanding it to gather

Jews, Samaritans, and Gentiles throughout the world. In fact, Acts 1:8 serves as the itinerary for the mission of the apostolic Church in Acts of the Apostles: "You shall be my witnesses in Jerusalem and in all Judea and Samaria and to the end of the earth." The apostles follow this fourfold expansion plan, first gathering Jews in Jerusalem (Acts 2-7), then having their followers evangelize in Judea and Samaria (Acts 8), and finally reaching out to the ends of the earth, primarily through the missionary journeys of St. Paul (Acts 9-28). Thus it is through Jesus and his Church that God's promise to bless all nations through Abraham's descendants is finally fulfilled.

CHAPTER 13

Getting Started: Translations, Resources, and Methods

Now it is time to launch. In the previous chapters we laid the foundation for how to interpret the Bible and addressed basic questions about the canon of Scripture, the trustworthiness of the Bible, the biblical world, and the Bible's "big picture." This chapter is intended to help equip readers to begin studying the Scriptures on their own. Here we will discuss some of the important resources and methods with which one needs to be familiar in order to get off to a good start in studying the Bible.

Which Translation?

Why are there so many translations of the Bible? What are the differences, and which one is the best? With so many translations of the Bible to choose from, one of the first fundamental questions a student of the Bible must face is: "Which version should I use?"

The Bible was written in three languages: Hebrew, Aramaic, and Greek. Most of the Old Testament was written in Hebrew, with some deuterocanonical books written in Greek and some other passages written in Aramaic, a Semitic language related to Hebrew that was used for international affairs in the ancient Near East and was increasingly used by the Jews after the Exile.

With the rise of Greek culture in the third century BC, Greek became the international language. Many Jews in the first century spoke Greek, and when the New Testament authors wrote their works, Greek was the main language used. Hence the ancient New Testament manuscripts were written in Greek, with the exception of a few passages that present Christ's words in Aramaic, the language he spoke.

At many points in history, the Bible has been translated into the common language of the people reading and hearing it. Even before Christ, the Old Testament was translated into Greek in the third century BC to serve the needs of the Greek-speaking Jews dwelling in Egypt. This translation, known as the Septuagint, became widely used especially among Jews outside Palestine and was used much by the New Testament writers themselves. (For more on the Septuagint, see Chapter 9.) Similarly, when Aramaic became the common language spoken by Jews in Palestine, the custom arose in the synagogues of offering the people an Aramaic paraphrase and explanation of the Scriptures read in Hebrew that day. These Aramaic paraphrases of the Bible were called *targums* (see Chapter 11).

In the early Church, as Christianity spread to non-Greek-speaking peoples, the Bible was translated into Latin and Syriac as early as the second century. It later came to be translated into diverse languages such as Coptic, Armenian, Ethiopian, and Old Slavic. The most famous translation of the Bible is the Latin Vulgate, which became the norm in Western Christendom for more than a thousand years.

In the English-speaking world, two translations of the Bible dominated the landscape for almost four hundred years: the King James Version (1611) for Protestants and the Douay-Rheims (1609-1610) in the Catholic tradition. However, since the mid-1940s, a plethora of new English translations have emerged. The dramatic increase in new versions is partly the result of a greater desire among Christians to have a translation based on more ancient and reliable manuscripts that are now available. Moreover, as many new

Greek texts from antiquity have been discovered, scholars have gained a better understanding of the Greek language and are thus in a position to make a more accurate translation of the Bible than in past generations. Finally, since the English language itself has evolved, older translations use words or phrases that are no longer commonly used or that have changed meaning, thus leading to difficulties in understanding. All this has led many scholars and Christian leaders to call for new translations of the Scriptures.

Meaning or Precision? Two Approaches to Translation

There are two main approaches to translating the Bible: 1) *formal correspondence* (or "formal equivalent") translations are more "literal" or "word-for word" translations that seek to correspond as much as possible with the grammatical structures and lexical forms of the original Hebrew and Greek manuscripts; and 2) *functional or dynamic equivalent* translations aim to communicate the original meaning of the biblical text, but are not as concerned about maintaining the grammatical structures, lexical forms, and idioms of the original text.

Here are some Scriptural examples to illustrate the differences between these two approaches. The RSV translates Acts 11:22 "News of this reached the ears of the Church at Jerusalem." As a formal correspondence translation, the RSV follows the Greek more closely and maintains the idiom in the Greek text about the Church having "ears." In contrast, the Good News Bible, as a dynamic equivalent translation, tries to communicate the meaning of this idiom and avoid expressions that might be awkward in modern English. Thus, the Good News Bible drops the image about the Church having ears and offers a simpler translation that communicates the sense of this verse: "The news about this reached the Church in Jerusalem."

Both approaches have value. Dynamic equivalent translations tend to be easier to read since they sound more natural in modern English and seek to offer the reader more assistance in understanding the meaning of the text. One shortcoming, however, is that these translations more often reflect the opinion of what some scholars say about the meaning of the text, leading readers to a particular interpretation which may or may not correspond to the original meaning itself.

Since no two languages are the same, all translations involve some level of interpretation. But the formal correspondence approach attempts to remain closer to the original text, even if that means keeping certain idioms or expressions that are a bit awkward in modern English. This approach is comfortable leaving various interpretive options open and allows readers to explore the meaning of the text themselves. Thus the formal correspondence approach is helpful for more serious study of Scripture, since it makes it easier to examine the structure of the original text and notice the sacred writers' literary techniques such as word play, verbal allusions, and repetition of key words, which are more often left out in dynamic equivalent translations.

Some popular formal correspondence translations include the Revised Standard Version (RSV), the Revised Standard Version-Catholic Edition (RSV-CE), the Douay-Rheims, and the New American Standard Bible (NASB). Popular dynamic equivalent translations include the New Jerusalem Bible (NJB), the Good News Bible (GNB), and the New English Bible (NEB). "In-between" translations, i.e., those that employ principles from both approaches, include the New American Bible (NAB) and the New International Version (NIV). Of these, the following are Catholic translations: the New American Bible (NAB), the New Jerusalem Bible (NJB), the Douay-Rheims, and the Revised Standard Version–Catholic Edition (RSV-CE).

Tools & Resources

A carpenter needs good tools in his toolbox. Similarly, students of the Bible need a number of good resources that can aid their study of the sacred books. Biblical dictionaries, a concordance, biblical commentaries, an atlas, and the *Catechism of the Catholic Church*, are among the many tools that can help students know and understand the Scriptures better. Most of these can be purchased in printed form at Christian bookstores or online. And some are even available as online resources now.

Bible dictionaries and biblical encyclopedias offer quick, helpful information about the history, geography, terms, people, places, customs, and events related to the Bible. For example, if one wants to learn more about the various sacrifices in the Old Testament, most biblical dictionaries will have an article under the title "Sacrifice" that will discuss the historical origin of sacrifice in the Old Testament, the various kinds of sacrifices, their purpose, the meaning of the rituals associated with sacrifice, and references to many key biblical passages about this topic. Biblical dictionaries can come in one condensed volume or more extensive, multi-volume editions.

Concordances are valuable resources that index the major words and names in the Scriptures, providing the location (chapter and verse) for every occurrence of that word in the Bible. A concordance is an indispensable resource for locating all biblical references to a key word, name, place, or topic. For example, if one wants to know everything the Bible tells us about Mary Magdalene, one can look up in a concordance all the times she is mentioned in the Scriptures, and then look up and study those passages to gain a broader grasp of the role she plays in the story of God's plan of salvation.

Biblical commentaries examine a book (or books) of the Bible verse-by-verse or section-by-section, explaining a biblical text from a variety of angles. Most commentaries will expound on the significance of a text by discussing the meaning of the Greek or Hebrew words used, how an action or description would have been understood in its original historical context, the literary techniques used, how the Christian tradition and recent scholarship have interpreted a text, and how the text can be applicable to Christian theology and life today. Some commentaries are short, concise books, easy for lay readers to follow, while others are longer, academic works intended for scholars. Some are moderately detailed and intended for pastors, teachers, and the more serious lay reader of the Bible.

Bible atlases provide a collection of maps from the ancient Near Eastern world of the Old Testament (focusing on Israel and her neighbors) and the wider Mediterranean world, especially of the New Testament period. Maps put the places, journeys, battles, exiles, and empires mentioned in the Bible in their proper geographic context. This can help us better understand, for example, Paul's missionary journeys or Judah's exile to Babylon or Christ's itinerant ministry in Galilee and his final journey to Jerusalem.

The *Catechism of the Catholic Church* is an indispensable resource for any Catholic studying Scripture. As we have seen throughout this book, Scripture is meant to be read in the heart of the Church. The *Catechism* offers a systematic presentation of the living tradition and the doctrines of the Church that help illuminate our understanding of the Bible (see Chapters 5 and 6). One can think of the *Catechism* as a systematic summary of the story of salvation. As such, it should come as no surprise that the *Catechism* itself is saturated with references to Sacred Scripture. Indeed, the Bible is the most referenced book in the *Catechism*.

One can use the *Catechism* for Scripture study in several ways. On a most basic level, the more one understands the Catholic faith, the better equipped he will be for reading Scripture. He will have a good sense of the faith, which will help guide his interpretation within the living tradition of the Church (see Chapter 5) and the analogy of faith (see Chapter 6). That is why studying the *Catechism* in general will enrich one's study of Scripture.

Moreover, the *Catechism* can show how the Catholic faith sheds light on a particular biblical passage. The back of the *Catechism* provides an index of all the Scriptural verses it references. For example, if one wants to know how the beatitudes in Matthew's gospel (see Mt 5:3-11) have been interpreted in the Church or used in Catholic morality or spirituality, this index points to the many articles in the *Catechism* that draw on and/or comment on these particular verses.

Finally, the *Catechism* provides an index of topics it covers. This can be a helpful guide for those wanting to explore how a topic touched upon in Scripture is developed in the Catholic tradition. For example, when studying the account of the Fall in Genesis 3, one may be interested in learning more about the Church's teaching on original sin. Or when reading about the resurrection of the dead in 1 Corinthians 15, one might be curious about what kind of body we will have at the end of time. The *Catechism's* topical index refers the reader directly to key paragraphs that explain these doctrines.

Methods of Study in Biblical Scholarship

Biblical criticism refers to the many tools and methods modern Scripture scholars use to examine biblical texts. These are called "critical" approaches not because they negatively critique the Bible, but because they are intended to help scholars study the Scriptures critically—that is, analytically—with various criteria to help them develop well-reasoned interpretations. In an attempt to be as objective as possible, these approaches apply to Scripture criteria similar to those employed by modern literary and historical scholars to examine other ancient texts.

In the world of biblical scholarship, these various approaches to biblical criticism fall into two main categories: historical criticism and literary analysis. Being aware of these methods will be particularly helpful when using many of the biblical resources mentioned above.

Historical-Critical Methods

The historical-critical method attempts to examine the history of a biblical text: how it came to be composed and how it was used in its original setting. It is called historical because it analyzes biblical texts in their original historical setting, examining "the historical development of texts or traditions across the passage of time." [85] It thus attempts to reconstruct the past, paying close attention to the history behind the text—the process of how the text came to be. Some of these historical-critical methods include *source criticism*, which studies the written sources that might underlie a particular biblical text. Like many authors today, the ancient biblical writers sometimes used previously existing sources in the composition of their works (see Nm 21:14-15; Mt 1:23; Lk 1:1-4). *Form criticism* identifies the various oral traditions behind a biblical text and examines their original setting in the life of the believing community. For example, certain material in a biblical text might have originally been used in an oral form such as a proverbial saying (e.g., Mt 6:24), a brief creedal statement (1 Cor 15:3-5), or a poem or hymn in the early Church (Phil 2:6-11; Col 1:15-20). Learning more about the oral traditions behind a biblical text can shed light on the meaning the passage originally had for the early Christians. *Tradition criticism* analyzes how these traditions grew, developed, and were knotted together over the course of time. *Redaction criticism* studies how a text arrived at its final form, analyzing how the final redactor of these traditions edited, arranged, and added to this material, and examining the editorial tendencies of the final redactor that might reveal his pastoral or theological purposes.

Historical Authenticity

Finally, scholars using historical criticism at times seek to investigate the historical accuracy of statements made in a biblical text. Though such an inquiry in itself can be valuable, the underlying assumptions and criteria that have sometimes been used in modern Scripture scholarship can be problematic. For example,

---

[85] Pontifical Biblical Commission (PBC), *The Interpretation of the Bible in the Church*, Introduction, A.

when studying the gospels, some scholars have approached the text with the presupposition that God does not interact in this world; therefore, there can be only natural causes for events. Such a commentator would conclude, for example, that when the gospels report Jesus healing someone or calming a storm—actions that violate the "laws of nature"—the biblical text cannot be relaying what actually occurred in history. Some other explanation for these miracle stories must be given: perhaps there was a natural cause for the event (Jesus used natural herbs or medicines to cure the person; the weather changed suddenly) or perhaps the Gospel writer invented the story in order to communicate a theological truth (Jesus has compassion on the sick; Jesus is powerful).

Some scholars also have at times used various criteria to evaluate the authenticity of a saying or action of Christ. For example, one criterion called *multiple attestation* requires a saying or event in the gospels to be reported by more than one source in order for it to be considered historical. Thus, according to this criterion, if a saying of Jesus is recorded in only one gospel, we cannot be confident that he really said it.

Other criteria have been used to try to increase confidence that the early Church did not modify or make up a saying of Jesus that is found in the gospels. According to the criterion of *dissimilarity*, for example, if a saying of Jesus in the gospels is different from Judaism and the early Church, then we can be more certain that it goes back to Jesus himself, since the Gospel writers would not have taken it over from the contemporary Jewish environment or from the beliefs and practices of the early Church. Such dissimilarity increases confidence that the saying is authentic.

These presuppositions and criteria can place unreasonable standards of historicity on the gospels and lead one to approach the texts with undue suspicion. For example, if a scholar automatically rules out the possibility of God interacting in this world, that unproven assumption will shape his assessment of the historicity of the miracle accounts in the gospels, for he brings his bias against miracles into his judgment about the biblical text. Moreover, by not being even open to the possibility of God interacting in this world, such a scholar holds a bias that not only is unreasonable (see Chapter 1), but also goes against the worldview of the original Christian writers and readers of the gospels, which he seeks to explain.

Similarly, while multiple attestations of a saying of Christ can reinforce our confidence in a gospel's account of that saying, the existence of only a single attestation should not in itself make the saying less historically authentic. And although the criterion of dissimilarity can help underscore what is unique about Jesus—how he is sufficiently distinct from the Judaism that preceded him and from the Church that came after him—it has a bias against any continuity between the Jewish environment from which Jesus emerged and the Church he founded. Since Jesus was a Jew with a ministry among the Jewish people, it seems highly unlikely that there would be no Jewish elements in his life, teaching, and mission. And it seems just as unlikely that the historical Jesus would be completely different from the Christian movement he founded.

Faith and History

Since biblical faith is about real historical events that took place in this world, historical study of the Scriptures is absolutely indispensable. But Pope Benedict XVI and others have cautioned that the historical-critical method in general has limitations.[86] It can assist readers in exploring the human dimension of Scripture, and it can help analyze the meaning of a text in its original historical setting and the process of how a text might have come to be in the original Jewish or Christian communities of faith. However, since Scripture also has a divine dimension and since the inspired biblical word speaks to people today, the Bible itself cannot be fully understood by historical-critical methods alone.

---

[86] See J. Ratzinger, *Jesus of Nazareth*, pp. xvi-xviii; PBC, *The Interpretation of the Bible in the Church*, I, A, 4 – I, B.

When the study of Scripture fails to adequately take into account the divine dimension, it remains a study of the past and cannot make the inspired word present to people today, Pope Benedict has argued. It also can lead to the denial of the divine acting in history. Pope Benedict, for example, notes how exclusive use of historical criticism has led some segments of "mainstream" biblical scholarship today even to deny that Jesus instituted the Eucharist or rose from the dead.

Pope Benedict thus emphasizes that historical-critical methods need to be complemented by the approaches that take into account the divine dimension of Scripture.[87] Along these lines, he has specifically mentioned the use of the four senses of Scripture (see Chapter 7) and the three criteria from Vatican II for interpreting Scripture—which involve being attentive to 1) the content and unity of the Bible; 2) the living Tradition; and 3) the analogy of faith (CCC 111-119) (see Chapters 4-6).[88] When the Bible is studied in this way, we read the Scriptures in light of the same Spirit in which they were written and have their treasures opened for us today.[89]

Literary Analysis

The second category of biblical criticism involves newer methods of literary analysis. These approaches do not make hypothetical reconstructions about how the biblical texts might have come to be. Instead, they study the literary features of *the biblical text as it stands in its final form.* Such studies are valuable because "it is the text in its final stage, rather than in its earlier editions, which is the expression of the Word of God."[90]

---

[87] See Pope Benedict XVI, *Address During the 14th General Congregation of the Synod of Bishops* (October 14, 2008); *Jesus of Nazareth,* pp. xvii-xx; PBC, *The Interpretation of the Bible in the Church,* I, A, 3 – I, B.

[88] See Pope Benedict XVI, *Address During the 14th General Congregation of the Synod of Bishops* (October 14, 2008); *Jesus of Nazareth,* pp. xvii-xx.

[89] J. Ratzinger, *Jesus of Nazareth,* pp. xv-xxiv.

[90] PBC, *The Interpretation of the Bible in the Church,* I, A, 4.

Some of the more recent forms of literary criticism include *narrative analysis,* which examines plot, characters, settings, and the narrator's point of view in order to demonstrate how a narrative tells its story. This approach has shed much light in recent scholarship on the Pentateuch and historical books of the Old Testament, as well as the gospels and Acts in the New Testament. *Rhetorical analysis* examines the rhetorical strategies used in the Bible and their persuasive effect on readers. This approach analyzes texts in light of classical Greco-Roman rhetoric and Semitic rhetorical and literary strategies. It has particularly contributed to our understanding of Paul's letters, Jesus' discourses in the gospels, and the apostles' speeches in Acts. *Semiotic analysis* (or *structuralism*) seeks the meaning of the biblical text found in the deep structures common to all stories (actors, times, places, types of actions, plot development). This method identifies and classifies each element of a story in order to discern the objective meaning of the story that, according to this approach, resides not in the author's intention or in the reader's response but in the structure of the text itself. Finally, the *canonical approach* interprets biblical texts not in isolation, but in light of the whole of Scripture as found in the canon that has been received as an authoritative norm by the believing community. Pope Benedict has argued that this approach is "an essential dimension of exegesis" for it carries out the Second Vatican Council's principle that Scripture should be studied in a way that is attentive to the content and unity of Scripture as a whole.[91]

---

[91]   J. Ratzinger, *Jesus of Nazareth,* p. xvii.

CHAPTER 14

Lectio Divina: Praying Scripture

While serious study of Scripture is important, it is not enough. Ultimately, we want God's word to penetrate our hearts and shape our lives. A Christian who memorizes the Scriptures and understands every doctrine in the *Catechism* would not necessarily be close to God. Certainly, we must understand the word of God intellectually, but we also must allow it to penetrate our hearts and bear fruit in our lives.

The Blessed Virgin Mary is a model for this interiorization of God's word. When Mary witnessed the amazing events surrounding the birth of her son, the Scriptures tell us that she "kept all these things, pondering them in her heart" (Lk 2:19; cf. 2:51). On a basic level, the notion of keeping and pondering in the heart indicates that she sought to understand the meaning of the mysterious events at the dawn of the New Covenant era (see Gn 37:11; Dn 4:28).

But the phrase tells us something more. In the psalms and wisdom literature of the Bible, to keep and ponder in the heart implies not just a correct interpretation of God's words and deeds, but a faithful living out of God's revelation. For example, Psalm 119:11 says, "I have laid up your word in my heart, *that I might not sin against you.*" Here, the psalmist ponders God's words in his heart so that he may live according to these words.

Therefore, we learn from Mary that it is not enough to know God's word in our minds. We must interiorize God's word and allow it to mold our lives. We need to take the Scriptures to prayer, meditate on them, and apply them to the situations we face each day. We, like Mary, should keep the word of God and ponder it in our heart, so that we may walk in his ways.

Divine Reading

One traditional method of praying with Scripture in a way that helps us interiorize it is called *lectio divina*. The Latin word *lectio* means "a reading" while *divina* means "divine." Thus, *lectio divina* is a divine reading of Scripture. It refers to the way great monks, saints, and mystics throughout the centuries have read the Bible in the context of personal prayer—in intimate dialogue with the God who speaks to us through his words in Scripture.[92]

The method of *lectio divina* was once summed up by the monk Guigo the Carthusian in four basic steps: reading, meditation, prayer, and contemplation. He described the fourfold method as four rungs on a ladder that lifts the soul toward heaven:

> *Reading* is the careful study of the Scriptures, concentrating all one's powers on it. *Meditation* is the busy application of the mind to seek with the help of one's own reason for knowledge of hidden truth. *Prayer* is the heart's devoted turning to God to drive away evil and obtain what is good. *Contemplation* is when the mind is in some sort lifted up to God and held above itself, so that it tastes the joys of everlasting sweetness.[93]

Reading is the most basic step, and also the most foundational.

---

[92] See Tim Gray, *Praying Scripture for a Change* (West Chester, PA: Ascension Press, 2008) for an excellent, practical introduction to *lectio divina*.

[93] Guigo the Carthusian, *A Ladder of Monks and Twelve Meditations* (Kalamazoo, MI: Cistercian Publications, 1979), pp. 67-8.

This involves examining the details of a passage, carefully observing what the text actually says. Here one pays close attention to the key characters, actions, words, and ideas presented in a biblical passage. Asking questions like a reporter can be helpful here: *Who? What? When? Where?* The goal of this first step is to apply one's mind to the text in order to take in as fully as possible simply what the Bible is saying.

Meditation involves reflecting on the meaning of the text. As the *Catechism* explains, in meditation, "the mind seeks to understand the why and how of the Christian life, in order to adhere and respond to what the Lord is asking."[94] After observing the details of the text in the first step of reading, the second step of meditation leads us to ask why the Lord put those details in the text. Why was a certain word or image used? Why did Jesus ask the paralyzed man, "Do you want to be healed"? What is the significance of the servants at Cana filling the water jars "to the brim"? Seeking the meaning of the details we observed in our reading of the text provides material for conversation with God in the next step, prayer.

Prayer is our conversation with the Lord about his words to us in Scripture. Here we ponder the Scriptures in our hearts, speaking with God. We may express how our meditation moves our soul. We may thank the Lord for how this passage manifests his goodness. We may ask the Lord for insight. We may seek to know how this passage applies to our lives, asking the Lord what he wishes to teach us in this reading of Scripture. Here our reading becomes an intimate dialogue with God about his own inspired words to us.

Contemplation is the final step, which represents the climax and fruit of our divine reading of Scripture. According to the *Catechism*, it is a wordless prayer in which the mind and heart focus on God's greatness and goodness in loving adoration. It is a loving attentiveness to God himself. Through *lectio divina*, we may come to a deeper understanding of God, his Church, or his plan for

---

[94] CCC 2705

our lives. When we perceive the beauty and goodness of God and his works of salvation, our souls are lifted up in awe, and we may experience deep peace and joy and an "interior knowledge of our Lord."[95] Contemplation does not have to be something profoundly extraordinary, reserved only for great saints and mystics. As St. Teresa once said, contemplation is "a close sharing between friends; it means taking time frequently to be alone with him who we know loves us."[96]

Indeed, this is what the dialogue between God's word to us in Scripture and our response in love and faith is ultimately meant to be: "a close sharing between friends."

[95] CCC 2715
[96] CCC 2709

INDEX

A

Abraham, 61, 63, 93, 95, 108, 111; call of, 112; descendents of, 117; God's promises to, 101, 116, 118-122; God's unveiling of himself to, 18; original home of, 100

Acts of the Apostles, 20, 30, 43, 45, 49, 96, 102, 104, 113-115, 121-122, 125, 134

Adam, 61, 107, 111, 116, 118; as a "type of Christ" 59; as the "heavely man" 108; temptation of, 112

Algebra, 15

Allegorical sense, 57, 108

Anagogical sense, 58

Analogy, 15, 43; of faith, 36, 51-52;128, 133

Anthony of the Desert, St. 1-2

Anthropology, 94

Antiochus Epiphanes IV, 121

Apocryphal, 76, 79, 81, 106

Apokalypsis, 16

Apostasy, 117

Apostles, the, 13 68, 70, 102; as "ambassadors for Christ", 54; as witnesses to Christ's kingdom, 122; authority of, 53-55, 81; Jesus'

command to, 19; Jesus greeting of *shalom* to, 30; Jewish world of, 107; successors of, 19, 45, 48, 53-55, 81; resurrected Christ's first words to, 29; hand on the Tradition of the Church, 45-46, 48-49

Aramaic, 7, 106, 109, 123-124

Archaeology, 3, 69; biblical, 93-96

Armenian, 124

Asia Minor, 98, 104

Assyrian, 99

Astronomy, 87

Athanasius of Alexandria, St., 68

Athlete, 96

Atlases, biblical, 128

Attestation, multiple, 131-132

Augustine, St., 1-2, 47, 90-91, 149

Authority, 49, 51, 53-55, 79-81, 85

Author, intention of the, 3, 9, 27-31, 35-36, 85-88, 134; as the first key to interpreting the Bible, 27

Authors, human, 8-9, 27, 30-31, 58, 86; intention of, 35-36, 85

B

Babylon, 98, 120, 128

About the Author

Dr. Edward Sri is provost and professor of theology and Scripture at the Augustine Institute in Denver. In addition, he serves as a visiting professor at Benedictine College in Atchison, Kansas, where he taught full-time for nine years.

Edward is the author of several books, including *The New Rosary in Scripture: Biblical Insights for Praying the 20 Mysteries* (Servant), *Men, Women and the Mystery of Love: Practical Insights on John Paul II's Love and Responsibility* (Servant), *Mystery of the Kingdom: On the Gospel of Matthew* (Emmaus Road), *Queen Mother: A Biblical Theology of Mary's Queenship* (Emmaus Road), *Dawn of the Messiah: The Coming of Christ in Scripture* (Servant), and, with Mark Shea, *The Da Vinci Deception: 100 Questions About the Facts and Fiction of The Da Vinci Code* (Ascension).

With Curtis Martin, Edward is a founding leader of the Fellowship of Catholic University Students (FOCUS). He regularly appears on EWTN, speaking on Scripture, apologetics, and the Catholic faith. Edward holds a doctorate from the Pontifical University of St. Thomas Aquinas in Rome. He resides with his wife, Elizabeth, and their five children in Littleton, Colorado.